Overcoming Task Inertia

Jonathan Locke

Table of Contents

v

Introduction

Most books on motivation and productivity are written by what I call Type A personalities: go-getters and over-achievers. They have been working 16 hour days since the age of 16, achieved great success, and now wish to tell the world how to replicate that success. Unfortunately, I don't believe that many of them understand why they have been successful, even if they know what has made them successful.

I'd put myself into the under-achiever category. I could sometimes do incredible work, but I found it difficult to be consistently productive. I knew that I had the capacity for more, but wasn't working to my full capacity.

This was a source of immense frustration for me. I spent a good deal of my adult life searching for that perfect job that would motivate me to work hard, and never found it.

Fortunately, I discovered task inertia theory. Task inertia explained why I had been inconsistent, and what the root cause of my productivity problems were. By understanding it and how it applied to me, I was able to raise my consistent productivity to previously unheard of levels. But I'll tell you more about my story in the next chapter.

Task inertia is the mental resistance that we encounter when our brain tells us we need to do something. It is that little voice in our head that tells us this task could be done later, or is too boring, or that perhaps we should check social media instead. In this book, I refer to having high task inertia as having high mental resistance, making it difficult to get work done.

Many high-performing individuals that I've spoken to identify as having high task inertia, and they all cope with it in different ways. One friend had to wait until he was in a last minute panic before he was motivated to study for exams. Another friend structured his work day around when he knew he would be motivated enough to work.

Everyone I've spoken to agrees that task inertia has a negative impact on their lives, and they wish that they had a greater degree of control over their productivity. "Why can't I work when I want to work?" is a question that I frequently hear.

The bad news is that task inertia is the result of circuits in your brain that are habituated to firing in a certain way. You might call them ingrained habits or ways of thinking. This makes them difficult to change.

The good news is that modern science has revealed that our brains are more changeable than we previously believed, and with conscious effort, you can literally rewire your brain in the manner of your choosing. This book reveals new ways of thinking and new strategies for you to apply that will enable you to change your brain for the better.

Most books on productivity discuss the importance of keeping high motivation. Unfortunately, I have found that motivation is not sufficient when dealing with high task inertia. The combination of high motivation and high task inertia can produce intense frustration, as you have the desire to be productive, but your brain resists your efforts to do so.

Some of the advice given is extremely unhelpful, along the lines of "Just do it and you'll feel better". If I could just do it, I wouldn't be reading a book about motivation, would I? Motivation, while important, seemed to me to be only half of the story of what creates productivity. I knew that there was something else going on in my brain that made it difficult for me to be productive. Task inertia is that other thing, and provides insight into why my productivity is as high or as low as it is at any given moment.

It is important to differentiate between task inertia and motivation. According to dictionary.com, motivation is the cause or reason to act or accomplish something, frequently due to some inducement or incentive. Let's settle on a simpler definition, which for our purposes can be the desire to accomplish something.

When you have high motivation and high task inertia, you feel the urge to get things done but find it difficult to get yourself to sit down and do the work. This causes frustration and guilt. Many high performing people that I have spoken with identify with this problem, but until now, there has been no distinction between task inertia and motivation.

Defining the problem of productivity in more detail, using task inertia to explain what is happening, helps us to understand what is happening in the brain, and that understanding allows us to come up with helpful and targeted solutions that, over time, can lead to permanent changes in the brain.

I have battled with high task inertia for my entire life. It has made it far more difficult for me to just get things done. But, thanks to task inertia theory, I finally understand why I have struggled, and this has made it possible for me to develop coping strategies to overcome my high task inertia.

This book will explain what task inertia theory is and how it frustrates your efforts at being productive. Through reading it, you may gain a better understanding of why you struggle to work as hard as you would like to. You will also learn new ways of thinking and habits that may be effective at managing or reducing your task inertia, enabling you to have the output you have always dreamed of.

But before we get into that, let's get into a few misconceptions about productivity.

Motivation and task inertia

Motivation is a critical factor in productivity. Task inertia theory does not ignore motivation, nor does it treat motivation as unimportant. Rather, task inertia theory attempts to explain why someone can have high motivation and yet still be unproductive.

Motivation operates at a higher level than task inertia does. Motivation is concerned with more general themes and longer outcomes than task inertia is. Task inertia is more of a pattern of behaviour than it is an attitude towards work. Motivation relates to one's general attitude towards the body of work, and is affected by organisational culture, relationships with colleagues, and incentives or disincentives.

Both motivation and task inertia fluctuate over time. However, high task inertia tends to be a behaviour pattern that makes its presence known when motivation drops below a threshold. Unfortunately for sufferers of task inertia, this threshold is relatively low, meaning that sufferers frequently cycle between productive and unproductive.

Perceptions of productivity

Productivity is a taboo subject in the workplace. Discussions of productivity are frequently guarded and defensive, as people worry about how they will be perceived if they admit to struggling to be productive. People will freely admit to lower productivity due to matters outside of their control, but will only hesitantly admit to not being productive because of personal struggles.

One of the key reasons for this is the perception that if you struggle to concentrate on your work, you are lazy. Laziness is said to be a sin, a sign of lacking motivation, or "not wanting it enough". Therefore, people with productivity problems will say whatever they can to avoid being labelled as lazy.

I dislike labelling people in this way as I feel it offers no possibility for improvement. Labelling somebody as lazy is itself a lazy activity, in that it involves no real attempt to understand why the person is unproductive in the first place.

An accusation of laziness is inherently judgmental, and I feel that being judgmental will shut down any growth of trust and understanding, which are so crucial to good employment relations. Moreover, I believe it is ineffectual. Accusing somebody of laziness is about making yourself feel superior for your own amazing work habits, not offering someone a chance to improve on their productivity.

If you are reading this book, you are likely to not be lazy at all. You might have internalised the belief that you are lazy due to years of being labelled as such. However, if you feel motivated to work, and yet still struggle to get anything done, it might be due to task inertia.

Working all the time

The aim of this book is not to turn you into someone that can work 100 hours per week. Nor does this book aim to turn you into someone that wants to work 100 hours per week. This book aims to help you become as productive as you can within the time that you allocate for working. Whether that is 1 hour or 100 hours, the choice is yours.

Society frequently places large expectations on us to work longer and longer hours. In some circles, it is seen as a badge of honour to spend nearly every waking minute working, "hustling", or chasing the next big thing. That isn't what I want in my life, and that's okay. All I want is to be able to do a solid day's work and feel good about it, and not have tasks run over because I was distracted.

This book also aims to raise your happiness about working, by reducing the stress that you associate with working. This will come about because of an increase in productivity without a corresponding increase in hours worked. You'll get more done, and you'll feel good about yourself for having done so.

By the end of this book, I want you to be able to choose when and for how long you work, instead of sitting at your desk distracted, feeling like you're going out of your mind. This will lower your stress while also enabling you to get more done, all without needing to actually spend longer working.

ADHD and task inertia

This book is not intended to assist in diagnosing or treating ADHD. If you believe you may have ADHD, I recommend speaking with a health professional who will better be able to assist you.

Early on in my search for answers, I thought I might have ADHD myself. I read up all about the symptoms. It seemed to explain a lot - why concentrating on my work was so difficult. I hoped that I'd have the diagnosis confirmed, and then could manage it according to best practices as recommended by trained health professionals.

But, a psychiatrist told me that I didn't meet the criteria for diagnosis of ADHD. This was because outside of work, I had no problem concentrating at all. I could read for hours without getting distracted if I wanted to, and if I needed to, I could focus on my work. But it usually took a deadline to provide me with the focus I needed.

Task inertia provides the answer as to why I found it so difficult to concentrate on my work - it was because the inertia for all of my work tasks was too high for my brain to want to do them.

The strategies contained in this book definitely helped me manage my high task inertia, and they may also help if you are diagnosed with ADHD. However, I would still recommend speaking with a health professional prior to making any changes.

Who is this book for?

I come from a software engineering background, having been a software engineer for over 13 years. It is natural then that this book includes much from my own experiences as a software engineer. A software engineering job involves a lot of concentration on difficult tasks, and not all of these tasks are interesting.

You might be wondering then if task inertia theory applies to people who are not in software engineering roles. The answer, from conversations I've had with colleagues and peers who are not software engineers, is that it does. Task inertia can apply to any role which involves tasks that require a lot of concentration. Being a student is not a role in the sense that it does not constitute employment, but studying tends to require a lot of concentration, and so it is affected by task inertia too.

As we'll see later, whether or not task inertia applies depends on the individual. Some people may have even switched careers to something that requires less concentration, in order to minimise the impact of their task inertia.

If you don't identify as a task inertia suffer, this book may still help you improve your productivity through general advice as well as strategies and routines that are proven to be effective.

Chapter Summary

- Task inertia is the mental resistance we feel when trying to get work done.

- Task inertia and motivation both affect productivity.

- Task inertia relates to working habits and patterns of behaviour more than attitudes, rewards or incentives.

- Task inertia is not ADHD, and ADHD is not task inertia.

Chapter 1

History of task inertia theory

Task inertia theory came to me out of necessity, during the lockdown imposed to manage the COVID-19 pandemic. I had been working from home for a few months, and my productivity was as low as it had ever been.

I'd feel the urge to get things done, but I'd be unable to do anything. I'd sit in front of my computer and browse the Internet rather than work. I realised that I found the Internet boring, but browsed it anyway, to escape from work.

This frustrated me to no end. I know how much better I feel when I have done a decent day's work. Despite that, I just couldn't make my mind perform the tasks necessary to accomplish anything.

Not working when I knew that I could and should work harder caused me to feel guilty, and this caused me a lot of stress. Needless to say, the stress did not make my productivity rise any higher.

I warily discussed this with some of my colleagues. Some of them mentioned that they had become great at presenteeism but bad at long term tasks. In other words, they would respond to messages within seconds, no matter the time of day, in order to give their colleagues the impression that they were working hard. Perhaps also to make themselves feel better. But, they found it difficult to concentrate on long term tasks without immediate deliverables.

I was wary because of the taboo of discussing productivity. Most of us would rather not admit that some days, we were unable to get any real work done because we could not concentrate. We'd rather tell our colleagues that we have a difficult time switching off after a day of work, because we're so energised and so excited by how we can add value to our employer's business. But we have difficulty admitting that we struggle to be productive, struggle to cope, and feel guilty because of that. This is because our culture sends us the message that productivity is entirely within our control, and if we don't work hard, it is because we are lazy. Needless to say, I believe this attitude to be worse than unhelpful.

I found myself behaving the same as my colleagues, responding to Slack messages at any time of day, but feeling like I was getting little real work done. In fact, I felt, and still feel, that I was doing even less long term work than my colleagues. Work piled up, self-made deadlines slipped, and with it, my stress levels climbed. Guilt caused stress, stress caused productivity to decline further, and that caused yet more guilt.

One day, I came across an article (*) written by Erin Power about making the most of quarantine during the COVID-19 pandemic. It argued that people tended to offer advice that falls into one of two camps – either you should rest and take it easy on yourself, or, you should be hustling as much as possible. The author disagreed with both approaches, and instead advocated doing whatever is right for you, whatever that may be. That encouraged me to think a little deeper about the solution to my problem, and what would truly be best for me.

I realised that I needed to fix my productivity problems in order for my stress and guilt levels to decline, and my mood to improve. It wasn't so much that I minded wasting the time afforded by the lockdown, it was that the guilt and stress were eating me alive and I needed to improve my productivity to lower both of them. Improving my productivity thus became a necessity to me - I simply could not carry on as I was before.

I had reached such a low point that I had no choice but to improve my productivity. I could not carry on as I was before. I realised that lockdown was likely to persist until the end of 2020 at the very least, and that meant I could not hope for a quick return to normalcy and productivity. I had to figure out how to be productive at home, or else I risked worsening stress levels and productivity with no end in sight.

I'd struggled with inconsistent productivity for my entire working career. The amount of work that I'd be willing to do seemed to fluctuate heavily, but now that I was stuck at home with no boss peeking over my shoulder, my productivity fell to its lowest level in some time. Worse, I realised that because of the pandemic, we were not going to be allowed back in the office for some time. Therefore, this was not something I could simply wait out.

It was the realisation that I relied upon the external structure provided by a boss in order to be productive that propelled me towards a solution. External structure refers to any system that creates a sense of obligation in you to do your work. An example could be a manager that checks whether you have done your work, or a timekeeping system that raises a red flag if something is not done on time.

This is not to say that any lack of work on my part would not have been noticed. It would have, but the feedback may only have been provided some time later. This is because, in mature working environments, the assumption is that employees are self-motivated enough to do their own work without needing constant reminders.

At the age of 35, I could not ask my boss to micromanage me in order to raise productivity. Neither would I want to. I started to wonder if I could trick my brain into thinking there was an external structure that could create accountability.

I researched habits, which were said to be effective antidotes to productivity problems. While habits helped in some areas, they did not provide all of the improvement I was looking for (see Chapter 7 for more information on habits). I had to find the cause of my lack of productivity in order to move forward.

It was then that the idea of task inertia theory came to me. I realised that it could not be as simple as lacking motivation, being lazy, or social media. Something else was going in my head that made it difficult for me to begin work.

Task inertia theory explained everything neatly. It allowed me to understand why I had battled for so long and also what I needed to do to fix the problem. Simply put, mental resistance to performing tasks is caused by being more concerned with how performance of a task makes you feel rather than the outcome of a task. But other factors affect task inertia, which we will get into.

Why had I developed such high task inertia when my own brothers had not? Its impossible for me to say with certainty now, but I believe that task inertia develops over time as a result of bad work habits.

I was a smart child and teenager. My mother said she knew I was intelligent because I figured out how toys worked before anyone else did. I was a good if slightly unremarkable student in primary school, but in high school, things changed. I began to excel. I aced everything with no effort. Soon I was coming top of my class.

I'd always pay attention during class, but if I tried to study for exams, I found that I got horribly bored. We'll examine this in more detail later, but you should recognise that it took external structure - a teacher - to make me work. I knew everything already, and reading it over again wasn't going to make it stick deeper in my brain.

I still aced everything. After a routine IQ test when I was 14 years old, the guidance teacher asked me if school was easy. It was, no question about it. Even in my final year exams for high school, I didn't spend more than an hour in total studying for any of my exams. The material was just too boring to read. I still placed first in my class.

At university, I was proud of my ratio of work to results. In fact, at university, my lecture attendance decreased where I could get away with it. I barely went to any accounting lectures, nor did I do many of the assigned practicals, and still passed with ease. Patterns like this continued through my university career. If I liked the subject, as I did computer science, I could get a distinction just by going to lectures, with no studying required.

What I want to draw your attention to is the pattern of behaviour that is visible. I didn't study, but still got good results, thus reinforcing my belief that there was no benefit to studying. But, this applies to work too. Therefore, my brain reinforced the idea that I need not work unless the work is interesting enough.

At least, this is my hypothesis. There is no way of knowing for sure, and frankly, the answer doesn't really matter as much as what I choose to do about it. In any case, it creates a problem for me, because my work habits cause productivity problems for me, which increases my stress.

The problem is that, when we get into the real world, even the best job includes some tasks that are not enjoyable. The idea that you will find a job that you enjoy every second of every day is unfortunately unrealistic. I spent my entire career searching for that one perfect job, and I never found it. What is worse is that I don't think I ever came any closer to finding it. It was during the COVID-19 lockdown that I finally realised there was no perfect job to be found, and that I'd have to create the perfect job by aiming to perfect how I performed my tasks.

While I aced high school and did well in university, I struggled in the real world. I struggled to reach the potential I knew I was capable of. I wanted to achieve more, I wanted to have that recognition that I was used to receiving in high school, but without hard work, it wasn't coming to me. I was convinced that this was because I just hadn't found the right job to motivate me, to pull that hard work and determination out.

So I searched in vain. I worked in many different jobs. I was made redundant in 2009. I studied a graduate diploma in industrial engineering, thinking that what I really needed was a new career track. It wasn't. What I really needed was to dig deep and pull myself out of this hole.

Fortunately or unfortunately, I could manage as I was. I wasn't happy, but neither was I desperate. I made a good income. Sometimes I worked hard, sometimes I did not. Sometimes I excelled, but mostly I was bright if unremarkable.

But when the lockdown associated with COVID-19 hit, I was plunged into the worst professional crisis I had ever known, and that left me with only one option - fix the problem.

Fortunately, I did. The result is the book that you are reading.

Chapter Summary

- Task inertia theory was developed out of necessity by me during the COVID-19 lockdown.

- Task inertia can make guilt and stress form a vicious cycle.

- Task inertia is characterised by relying upon external factors to be productive.

References

* - Power, Erin. (2020, May). *Ask a Health Coach: Setting Goals, Breaking Bad Habits, and Making the Most of the Quarantine.* Retrieved from https://www.marksdailyapple.com/setting-goals-bad-habits/

Chapter 2
Task inertia theory in depth

Now that you understand my history and what led me to develop task inertia theory, let's delve into the theory itself a bit deeper.

As I explained before, task inertia is the mental resistance that one feels when attempting to perform a task. It is separate from, but influenced by, motivation. Task inertia is the little voice in your head that gets you to procrastinate, causing stress for you later.

In order for task inertia theory to be useful for us, we have to build it into a model that we can use to predict human behaviour. Once we can do this, we can use the predictions of the model to understand why we behave a certain way. We can also use this information to begin to reduce our high task inertia to enable us to have the level of productivity that we have always wanted.

The broad questions that we would like the model to answer are:

- What is task inertia?

- How does task inertia influence productivity?

- How does task inertia interact with motivation?

- What factors influence task inertia?

- Is there an underlying cause of task inertia, and if so, what is it?

- How does task inertia influence task selection?

Therefore, we will create two smaller models that will help to answer both questions. Don't worry - despite the terminology used, this will not be overly mathematical or scientific!

Through discussing this model, you will gain a greater understanding of task inertia. At the moment, it may seem a little fuzzy, but once you have read this chapter, it will all make sense. You will understand task inertia by its effects on you and your work.

What is task inertia?

Hopefully by now you will be starting to understand what task inertia is, but in order to make it a little more clear, I'll go into more detail on task inertia itself before examining how it interacts with task selection, productivity and motivation.

We already know that task inertia is the mental resistance you feel when attempting to perform a task. But, it is important to note that task inertia only exists in the context of specific tasks. Basically, any time that you don't really feel like doing something, you will feel resistance to doing it, and this resistance is task inertia.

You will never feel resistance to doing tasks that you enjoy, even if they are work. My brother loves doing physical labour. It is how he relaxes. He likes fixing broken machines, mowing the lawn, and repairing furniture. To me, those are all chores. I'll do them if I have to, but I'll need motivation to do them. Therefore, I experience task inertia when trying to do chores, although luckily not too severe. He experiences no task inertia when thinking about mowing the lawn, because he enjoys it.

Therefore, task inertia is specific to the person, and also specific to the task. No two people will have identical task inertia for their respective tasks.

Most people reading this book will experience task inertia related to work, and I'd expect that this is the primary reason why they are reading this book. But, you could also experience task inertia with other things, such as exercise or meditation. Whether or not you experience task inertia for a specific task depends on how you feel about that task.

We can examine the task inertia of a specific task, but we can also examine the task inertia of a person with regards to their work. This allows us to discuss their task inertia in a general sense.

Task inertia is ultimately caused by the way that you think about work. It is driven by the mental habits that you engage in, when thinking about and doing work. This means that your average task inertia is driven largely by the way that you think about the work that you do. We will explore more of this later in the chapter.

Task selection

How do people select which tasks to perform? The answer is that they select a task which has less task inertia than their current task energy. This means that if your task energy is lower than the task inertia of your work tasks, you won't do any of them.

Let's break that down a little. We already know what task inertia is. Task energy simply refers to how much energy you are willing to spend on working at that moment. Various factors can affect how much task energy you have, and it changes from day to day, and in fact can change from moment to moment. You might have more task energy if you slept well and are in a good mood, but you might have less task energy if you are feeling upset or unwell.

Your task energy acts as the threshold that determines what you're willing to do. If you're feeling energetic and in a good mood, you might have lots of task energy, and be productive. If you're distracted, tired, or emotionally upset, you might have low task energy, and this will mean you won't feel like doing any of your work.

In simple terms, the reason for this is that you compare the task inertia of tasks that you're thinking about to your current task energy, and if your task energy is too low, you won't engage with the task. This is because not all tasks have the same task inertia. You might be feeling energetic enough to mow the lawn, but you do this because you don't feel like studying. This is because, at that moment, your task inertia for studying is too high.

So individual tasks have their own task inertia, and their task inertia can change over time. As we'll see later, various factors influence task inertia. The most famous one is of course deadlines. If you have an exam the next day, you are generally able to study, because that feeling of last minute panic sets in.

If you have low task energy, everything is an effort, and you will want to do the least taxing tasks such as sleep or browse social media.

This is why you feel such mental resistance when you want to start a task that you know you ought to. This is also why, even if you manage to start the task, it can be difficult to sustain the effort long enough for it to be finished. Your brain will fight you every step of the way because of the high task inertia.

Out of the possible tasks that you can do, the one you actually will depend heavily on context. If you're sitting at your computer trying to work, you might be tempted to browse the Internet. If it is a Saturday and you know you ought to be writing that book, you might be tempted to mow the lawn.

Another interesting thing that can happen is that you perform a productive task that unfortunately has nothing to do with your immediate needs. Imagine you have an important exam tomorrow. But, the task inertia for studying is higher than your task energy, so you won't study. However, you do have a strong wish to be productive. Thus, you might clean up your room or your house, because this is a productive activity. A part of your brain is satisfied that you are being productive, while you know that you are being productive at the wrong thing.

Does motivation increase task energy or does it decrease task inertia? It increases task energy but leaves task inertia relatively unaffected. So, high levels of motivation will increase your task energy, and this can help you be more productive.

You've probably noticed this when you started a new job. Eager to please, you worked long hours, to create a good impression. But then once you knew you had made it, you slacked off a little. Your motivation declined to normal levels, and with it, your productivity dropped. The problem is, your productivity drop was sharper than you might have expected. Why is this?

This is because task inertia is the product of long term work habits, and so is fairly difficult to change. While your motivation was high, your task energy was also high. This meant that your task energy was over the threshold of your task inertia, and you were productive. The problem is, as you noticed, as soon as your motivation declines to normal levels, your task energy declines with it. When your task energy drops lower than the threshold of your task inertia, you lose productivity quickly.

Social media

Social media is well known as a work disruptor. The current theory is that social media is incredibly addictive to our brains because of the small rewards that are generated when you interact with it. This reward is mediated by the neurotransmitter dopamine in your brain, and it was never designed to cope with social media. Hence, when social media appeared on the scenes, all of us became incredibly addicted to it.

However, I believe something else may be going on. When we apply task inertia theory to social media, we see that it almost always has near zero task inertia and a small perceived reward. This is because there is no effort or deadlines involved in using social media. You may feel a small reward when you see a funny meme or when someone likes your post. Thus, social media has incredibly low task inertia and always remains something your brain is willing to do.

You'll notice that if you have something more interesting or important to do, you can tune social media out quite effectively. If you are reading a good book, your desire to check social media drops considerably. If you have a deadline to meet, you won't check social media until after the deadline has been met.

Productivity

The next model we will discuss is the productivity model. This model predicts how productive an individual will be based on their level of motivation and their average task inertia. Note that we are concerned with the average task inertia which an individual experiences when trying to do their job, instead of task inertia specific to one task.

The short version is that productivity increases with higher motivation and decreases with higher task inertia. However, the interesting thing is that sufficiently high task inertia is able to cancel out high motivation. But let's delve into a little more detail in each factor.

Motivation

I gave a relatively concise definition of motivation in the introduction, which was:

"motivation is the cause or reason to act or accomplish something, frequently due to some inducement or incentive"

It is now time to discuss motivation in greater detail. First, we will be examining motivation in the context of work. The working context could be in formal employment or it could be entrepreneurial activity. It is important to note that motivation can arise from either internal or external factors. External factors are things not in the individual's direct control, such as the threat of being fired if they are late for work, or the promise of a bonus for being productive. Internal factors are wholly in the control of the individual, and include psychological drives that might compel one to work hard, such as the need for acceptance among one's peers.

Internal factors are more relevant to the entrepreneur, and this is why self-motivation is said to be an important characteristic of entrepreneurs. Both internal and external factors are relevant to the employee, and the degree to which they motivate an individual depends not only on the individual but also on the environment.

In general, motivation is necessary but not sufficient for the effort required to be productive. That is to say, without motivation, not much can be accomplished. But even with motivation, it is not certain that much will be accomplished - that depends upon task inertia.

Like internal motivating factors, task inertia is wholly in the control of the individual, and not visible to anyone else. However, they are not the same thing. One can have high internal motivation and high task inertia at the same time - a situation which will result in low productivity but endless frustration!

Your motivation will change over time. If you identify strongly with your organisation's mission and vision, you're more likely to be highly motivated. If you have a good leader managing you, you are also more likely to be highly motivated.

For people who don't suffer as much from task inertia, high motivation is all they need to be productive. But for those that do, unless their motivation is extremely high, their productivity suffers.

Internal motivation interacts with task inertia by changing task energy. However, internal motivation is not the inverse of task inertia, as while there is a correlation between the two, each can benefit from unique strategies of improvement. We'll discuss how high motivation can affect task inertia in more detail in the section on task selection.

In other words, in order to improve productivity, one can focus on internal motivating factors or one can focus on reducing task inertia. However, while internal motivating factors depend upon what one wants to accomplish, task inertia is generally the same for most work related activities. Therefore, reducing task inertia can benefit a wider range of activities than improving internal motivation.

Putting it all together, productivity is higher when motivation is higher, and lower when task inertia is high. High task inertia can be sufficient to cancel out all but the highest levels of motivation.

With all that said, we can now construct a model for predicting productivity. Our model is as follows:

Productivity = Motivation x inverse of task inertia

Don't be scared by the inverse there. It just means that, the higher task inertia is, the lower the productivity, and the lower task inertia, the higher the productivity.

This might be contrary to what you've heard. You've likely heard that "you just don't want it badly enough". You've probably heard that you just have to be more motivated. Is that really true? I know you can think back to a time when you were motivated, but still unable to work. I know I can. I'll tell you the story of how I became a writer and perhaps that will convince you.

I use Google Drive to store all of my writing work. I find it convenient because it syncs across all of my devices, is backed up to the cloud, and I can see how things have changed over time. The earliest piece of work that I have in Google Drive, unfinished of course, dates back to 2009. But by 2020, I had not published a single thing.

I have been working, inconsistently, on writing for over a decade, and not published anything. If it was motivation I lacked, I would have given up a long time ago. I don't believe that you can do something for over a decade and not be motivated by it. But, I also didn't actually publish anything in ten years, so clearly I wasn't very productive.

Motivated enough to work on writing for ten years and yet not productive enough to publish anything doesn't fit with the popular narrative, which is that if you don't work hard at something, it is because you don't want it badly enough. I don't agree with this, as my example shows.

To start making real progress with my writing, I had to understand task inertia and apply it to myself. When I did that, I was able to massively improve my productivity by lowering my mental resistance to work. At last, my productivity began to align with my motivation, and I made more progress in 6 months than I had made in the previous 10 years. This book is the result of that, and the result of discovering task inertia.

Factors that influence task inertia

Various factors can either raise or lower task inertia. These factors explain why a task that you accomplish without difficulty one day may become impossible the next day. The variation in these factors explains the variation in task inertia. Each of these factors may contribute to task inertia in greater or lesser degrees depending on the person and the situation.

External management structure

External management structure refers to having a manager who checks in regularly to see that work is done. This could be someone in the same office as you, or someone working remotely. Regular progress check-ins will increase your sense of urgency in performing your assigned tasks, because you know that someone is depending on the completion of those tasks. Your brain creates an obligation to have the work done for your manager, and thus, task inertia is lowered.

This can be quite an effective means of increasing productivity, and it is why having an accountability partner can help, even if they are not your manager. Many people have accountability partners to increase productivity in personal endeavours such as exercising and writing, and this is why that strategy is effective.

The downside with relying upon an external management structure is that it is external - if the management structure stops, is removed, or becomes less visible, productivity will suffer.

I noticed this in myself during the COVID-19 lockdown. When lockdown began, and I didn't go into the office anymore, I felt less pressure to get things done, and my productivity dropped.

Deadlines

Anyone who has ever suffered from task inertia knows that deadlines can make task inertia magically disappear. Suddenly your mind is clear and you can focus for as long as you need to. Your brain easily gets into a state of flow, during which time passes quickly, and you are wholly productive, not feeling the need to check social media or go down a Wikipedia rabbit hole.

The problem with deadlines is that they are imposed by external forces - typically an external management structure or a client. This means they are not in our control, which means that external factors have a greater degree of control over our productivity than we do.

Task novelty

Some tasks are more interesting than others, and we will tend to want to do the ones that we find interesting. This won't come as a surprise to many people.

Things that can make a task seem more interesting are whether we have done anything like that before, how challenging it is, and whether there is a short term reward for that task.

While I'm sure our managers would love to keep our work queues filled with interesting, novel tasks that are just challenging enough but not too challenging, the reality is that sometimes boring work needs to be done, and this is the case even if one is an entrepreneur and thus responsible for one's own work queue.

Interrupt Mode vs Concentration Mode

I like to break down types of work into two very broad categories - interrupt and concentrate. Interrupt work is when you are, well, getting interrupted by a colleague or a business partner, who needs something immediate. This occupies your attention, and because the interaction is real time, you'll engage with the tasks necessary and respond quickly.

Concentration mode, on the other hand, refers to tasks that are not immediately due, require you to concentrate, and must be done alone. Examples of concentration mode tasks include writing programming code (when not pair programming), writing any literature, or working on business documents.

What about meetings? I categorise meetings as occurring in interrupt mode, since the interaction is real time and involves other people.

It should not come as a surprise that people who suffer from task inertia do not exhibit task inertia when working in interrupt mode. It is only when they are forced to switch to concentration mode, that task inertia becomes apparent. For this reason, some task inertia sufferers gravitate towards jobs that require more interrupt mode tasks than concentration mode tasks. I even tried this out myself, but didn't meet with great success.

I was a product manager for 6 months. I thought that the interrupt mode work required would suit me well, and that I'd perform well. I wasn't entirely wrong – I was good at the communication part of the job. But, there are almost no professional jobs that involve purely interrupt mode work or purely concentration mode work. Inevitably, when I had to perform a concentration mode task, I still struggled with it. Worse, I didn't understand task inertia at the time, and so I didn't understand why I struggled. This created a cycle of guilt and stress, which worsened my productivity.

There are tasks that blur the line. Suppose that your manager comes to your desk and says that the production system is down, and you need to stop what you are doing and investigate the cause. Even if you are working alone to investigate the cause, and the task requires your full attention, the urgency of the task will likely make it easy for you to concentrate. This is related to the Deadlines factor of task inertia - you know the urgency of the situation, and this makes it easier for you to devote your full attention to the task.

You may have heard of something called the "flow state". Being in a state of flow refers to when a task occupies your entire concentration span. It is also called being "in the zone". You may experience this when you focus on something so much, that you lose track of time, you stop thinking about yourself, and you become completely absorbed in the task. The flow state is not limited to work - it can occur during sports, or music practice, as well as during work tasks.

How is the flow state different to concentration mode? Flow state is that wonderful feeling when we're completely absorbed in the moment. Concentration mode doesn't define how we're feeling when we're performing the task - whether we are fully absorbed or merely idling along. Concentration mode only refers to the fact that the work requires concentration in order to accomplish. If you're lucky, you will be able to get into a state of flow while doing concentration mode work, and that will enable you to get that work done quicker.

People with task inertia tend to struggle with concentration mode work, which can make it difficult for them to enter a state of flow. This is because entering a state of flow requires concentration. Their high task inertia can make it difficult for them to concentrate enough to enter a state of flow.

Common Examples of Task Inertia Causes

When we feel mental resistance to performing a task, there is often a little voice in our heads that tells us the reason why we have this mental resistance in the first place. If you learn to listen to your ghost about this, so to speak, you will be more in touch with the causes of your task inertia. Knowing the cause will then help you make changes to your working habits and improve your productivity.

However, I am going to share a spoiler, which is that often what that little voice in our head tells us is not helpful. We have got used to listening to it over the years that we no longer question it. When we understand what that voice is saying, we will then be able to critically analyse it.

This Work Is Too Boring

Everyone has had tasks that are simply boring. Various factors can make a task boring, from our lack of interest in the subject to the lack of challenge in the task. Task inertia sufferers often battle with boring tasks, because they find it more difficult to just push on and do the work. That is, unless there is a deadline looming.

This is a favourite of mine, and I've had this thought, and variations of it, in my head for a long time. Essentially, whenever I try to do a simple task that I already understand how to do, my brain tells me that this work is boring and I should not do it. Any work, once understood, becomes simple, and thus repetition can kill productivity for people with task inertia.

Many friends and colleagues have mentioned the same thing to me - work that is boring kills productivity. Whether it is studying something that they don't find interesting, or working on a boring task, the result is the same. Productivity crashes, and ekes along until the task is done or the deadline is over, whichever comes first.

You Can Do This Later

Simple, routine tasks, such as administration, can sometimes cause task inertia. We rationalise to ourselves that these tasks can be delayed, because the time taken to perform them is so negligible.

This would include cases where there is no urgency due to the lack of a deadline for the task. Since there is no deadline, or the deadline is far away, you feel comfortable postponing the work. In fact, your brain might irrationally underestimate how long the task will take to complete, just to get you not to do it. Even simple tasks can be underestimated, and so you frequently run past the deadline.

This tends to cause procrastination of administrative tasks such as capturing timesheets or the minutes of meetings. Since the task is not challenging and has little in the way of anticipated reward, we delay performing the task. Without good administrative hygiene, this can get us into trouble later, as we cannot remember the content of a meeting when we do finally capture the minutes for it.

If there is a quick and simple task that I understand how to do, my brain tells me I should put it off. Why do it now? It is so simple, you could do this task in your sleep. Wasn't there an interesting video on YouTube you wanted to watch? And so I put the task off, and reinforce the bad working habit.

Many people that I have spoken with share the same problem. This is why organisations sometimes have to enforce strict rules to ensure that timesheets are captured on time. Promoting good administrative hygiene is part of good governance, but unfortunately, many task inertia sufferers battle with administrative tasks.

This Work Is Too Difficult

Tasks that we find too difficult can trigger task inertia. Sometimes this is because they create hills in our minds that we don't have the energy to climb - their task inertia is greater than our task energy. Difficulty in this case could be because of the logical challenge of the work, but it could also be due to other challenges such as difficult conversations that need to be had. In some cases, you might attach negative emotion to a task that may lead to you avoiding it. One may be that you might wish to avoid having an emotionally draining conversation with a team member or client. You may wish to avoid breaking bad news to a client about a project. You may even disagree that a particular task is the right course of action.

It isn't necessarily that difficult tasks cause task inertia, it is that the difficulty provides an excuse for our brains to disengage. When this happens, it can be difficult to re-engage and push through the difficulty. Worse, if the difficulty is caused by negative emotion attached to a task, we frequently feel little reward for having completed the task. We anticipate a negative outcome and so delay the task.

Most of us will enjoy tasks with the right level of challenge - enough so that you feel you have accomplished something when you complete the task, but not so high that you feel frustrated. Anything out of that Goldilocks zone has the potential to cause our task inertia to engage strongly and put the brakes on. However, as you're aware, sometimes there are difficult tasks that need doing, and and we must take responsibility for them.

In my experience, task inertia frequently occurs when I reach a logically difficult point in a task, and my brain doesn't know what to do next. Rather than persevere and find a way through the problem, my brain tells me that I ought to check social media instead. Thanks brain for always having my back.

Common Themes

If you examine the three examples of task inertia above, you might notice that they have something in common. There are two things that they have in common, and if we examine these things, we can better determine what to do to improve our task inertia.

Ego investment

One of the things that these task inertia have in common is ego investment in the performance of the task rather than the outcome. I use the word ego to mean a sense of self, and not to indicate arrogance or vanity.

In all of the three examples of task inertia, the driving factor that governs whether we want to do a particular task or not is how that task makes us feel. While it is important to do work that you like, sometimes there are other equally valid reasons for needing to do a task. Among them could be that getting this task done will result in lower stress in the future.

Therefore, the primary cause of task inertia is that we involve our egos in the decision of what work to do.

People who suffer from task inertia invest their egos in the wrong place - in the tasks that they perform. People who do not suffer as much from task inertia tend to think about the task in the context of their long term goals, and this is where they invest their egos.

Doing so is what allows them to focus on work that you or I might consider boring or simple. The reality is that in the pursuit of our goals, all of us will at some point have to perform tasks that are boring or simple.

I won't speculate on why so many people suffer from task inertia. In my case, I believe it was brought on by my own bad working habits, reinforced over many years of schooling. However, the good news is that habits can be changed, especially when we understand the negative effects of the habit.

Internal vs external control

The hint for this one was the fact that external task management structure is a factor for task inertia. This indicates that we lack internal control over our actions, and instead, are largely driven by external factors. This is a problem, because without internal control over our actions, we'll get blown around by the wind, like a ship without a rudder.

It is true that even highly productive people are affected by an external management structure. External management structures would be ineffectual if they did not result in some organisation of productivity. But, the difference is that highly productive people don't rely upon external management structures for productivity. They create their own productivity, and this makes it easier for them to pursue any goal they like. They can work towards it on their own direction, without needing an external management structure to motivate them.

Psychologists call this having an internal locus of control if you believe that you are responsible for events in your own life, or having an external locus of control if you believe that you are largely affected by events beyond your control.

In the case of task inertia sufferers, it may not be a belief that you are consciously aware of. You may believe that you control the events in your life. But if you suffer from task inertia, it is likely that one area of your life that you have little control over, is whether you are productive or not. This lack of control means that you will be subject to changes in productivity that are outside of your control, and these changes can cause intense frustration and guilt. This guilt often occurs because we believe that our productivity is within our control, and yet despite that, struggle to be as productive as we would like.

Going forward

Investing your ego in the performance of a task and relying upon external control are the two primary causes of task inertia. Over the course of this book, you will become more aware that productivity can be brought under your control, and you'll learn several techniques to help you with this. You'll bring more intention with you into the work that you do, and take more responsibility for your productivity. You'll learn how to begin investing your ego where it belongs - in the outcome of tasks, rather than the performance of them.

Don't worry, you won't become a robot. It is still important to enjoy what you do. But you'll learn to temper your expectations, knowing that even the best job can be boring sometimes.

Chapter Summary

- Productivity is affected by both motivation and task inertia.

- You'll only perform a task if its task inertia is lower than your task energy.

- Various factors affect task inertia, including deadlines and novelty.

- There are two primary causes of task inertia:

- Investing your ego in the tasks you are performing rather than their results

- Relying upon external control over your productivity

Chapter 3

How task inertia affects different people

Not everyone is affected equally by task inertia. That is to say, we all have task inertia with some specific tasks, but for some of us, task inertia doesn't cause us any real problems. Whether your task inertia causes you problems depends largely upon your levels of motivation and how high your task inertia is.

We can categorise people according to their motivation levels and task inertia. It is useful to know that there are people that have low or non-existent task inertia because it means we can compare those who do have high task inertia with those who don't, and from that, figure out how to lower our own task inertia.

Thus, I have created three categories into which the majority of people will lie. It is important to note that with such broad categories, there are some people who might identify with more than one category. It is also important to realise that it is possible to move from one category to another depending on circumstances in your life. I have had stages in my life where I would have identified as being in each of the three categories, which I will discuss in more detail inside the categories themselves.

The three categories differ primarily in what drives their productivity. Unmotivated people - the first category - have little driving their productivity. They have such low motivation that nothing else matters to their productivity. While unmotivated people do tend to have high task inertia, you typically would not notice due to their low motivation. Conditionally productive people - the second category - have their productivity driven both by motivation and task inertia. However, their consistently high task inertia is what causes inconsistency in their productivity. Super productive people - the third category - suffer little if any task inertia, and their productivity is largely driven by motivation.

Below is a table that summarises what we will be discussing in this chapter. The above paragraph explains the basics, but some of this will only make sense once you have read this chapter. I recommend coming back to this table later.

Category	Motivation	Task inertia	Productivity	Stress
Unmotivated	Low	High	Low	Low
Conditionally productive	Fluctuating	Medium to high	Fluctuating	Medium to high
Super productive	High	Low	High	High
GOAL: Directionally productive	Fluctuating	Low	High	Low

The last category in the table – Directionally Productive – is our end goal, which I'll elaborate on after discussing the primary three categories. In short, we don't aim to become Super Productive, but merely to be as productive as we would like, when we would like to be productive. That requires getting our task inertia under control.

Most people reading this book will be conditionally productive. This is because unmotivated people don't care about improving their productivity, and super productive people aren't struggling with low productivity.

For each category, I will explain what the category means, what drives the performance of people in this category, and my experience from being in this category.

Unmotivated

Unmotivated people have chronically low motivation. Their internal motivation and drive is completely lacking. Their motivation is so low in fact, that their task inertia is relatively unimportant. That is to say, their low productivity is a consequence of their lack of motivation, and even the best work habits in the world would not render them productive.

In most cases though, low motivation does go together with high task inertia. Their low motivation frequently translates into poor working habits and very high mental resistance to doing any work.

The only way to get any work out of someone who is in the unmotivated category is to sit on them and micromanage them. Nothing else works. As soon as the micromanagement stops, the work stops. This is because their low motivation means they have very little task energy. External structure in the form of management is required to raise their task energy above the threshold at which work becomes possible.

I know this because that is how I was when I graduated from university. At my first and second jobs, I was solidly in the unmotivated category. I had no life goals. I had no career direction. I didn't care about whether I excelled at work. I just wanted to show up at work, get paid, and go home.

If I could get away with it, I would do as little as possible, including playing video games or reading books on company time. This was before the days of social media, which is probably fortunate because I think I would have watched YouTube all day.

I realise now that it wasn't my mental resistance to doing work that was the problem, it was that I didn't care whether I had any mental resistance to begin with. I didn't see it as a problem. I did have high task inertia, but it never caused me any guilt or stress because it didn't bother me that I wasn't productive.

I was intelligent enough and well studied enough to make it through interviews, but a thoroughly unproductive employee. I don't think there is much that either of my first employers could have done to get any work out of me.

But one of them did the best thing that they could have done - they made me redundant during the financial crisis of 2007-

2009. This caused me to sit up and take notice. I realised that I never would have been made redundant if I was a productive or valuable employee. This is not to say that productive or valuable employees have not been made redundant – clearly this does happen, and far more often than it should. It is merely to say that, being made redundant caused me to reflect honestly upon myself and my work ethic, and I realised I needed to improve.

Productivity Drivers

Low motivation and engagement drive productivity to very low levels. In fact, their high task inertia is of relatively little importance in determining their productivity.

This is because productivity is influenced in a multiplicative fashion by both motivation and task inertia. If either one is very low, productivity is very low. Productivity is only high when both are high.

Stress

Unmotivated people don't feel all that much job related stress. They are so unengaged that the only thing that stresses them out is the possibility of losing their job and having to find a new one.

In fact, this lack of stress is what sets them apart from conditionally productive people. Conditionally productive people feel more stress precisely because they are more engaged. With no engagement in their employer's goals, there is no transference of stress from manager to employee. Unmotivated people then coast through their jobs as long as they can.

Improving productivity

Improving the productivity of unmotivated people is difficult because their poor productivity stems from internal issues rather than external issues.

Therefore, in order to boost their productivity, one must attempt to influence their internal state, which would be difficult. You can see from my example above, that I had to be made redundant to begin questioning whether my values were in the right place.

In general, unmotivated people need to set personal goals in order to progress. In some cases, it may be that they need to go through a bad experience, like I did. In others, it could be that through self development they will realise that being chronically unmotivated is not a good way to get through life.

Conditionally Productive

Conditionally productive people experience varying motivation levels and medium to high task inertia. This means their productivity tends to vary with their motivation - hence conditionally productive. Their working conditions have to be just right for them to be productive, and they are unable to directly control their productivity themselves.

If a deadline is coming up, they can be highly productive. But with no deadline, poor motivation and no micromanagement, expected poor productivity even with high engagement.

After I was made redundant, I moved into what I call the conditionally productive phase. My motivation improved and so did my productivity, but I still had highly variable task inertia.

This made me very inconsistent. For a few months, if my motivation was high, I'd be a star performer, working at an incredible rate and never tiring. Then my task inertia would creep up, and my productivity would drop.

These cycles continued for years. More often than not, I was at the lower end of my possible productivity. This made me unhappy, and so I spent ages searching for a new job that would finally make me productive and happy. I studied a graduate diploma in industrial engineering thinking that I needed to get out of software engineering and into management because then I'd be productive.

None of that turned out to be true. I was going from job to job hoping to find the answer externally. But the answer was always internal. I just didn't know what task inertia was.

This book is written to help conditionally productive people. It is conditionally productive people who will see the most benefit from reading this book.

Productivity Drivers

Both motivation and task inertia influence the productivity of a conditionally productive person. However, their task inertia tends to cause greater inconsistency in their productivity.

This is because motivation can be expected to ebb and flow over time depending on the work conditions. However, some people can make it through the dips with only slight drops in productivity, whereas in others, an ebb in motivation causes productivity to plummet.

This is why the productivity of conditionally productive people tends to decline the longer they stay in a job. Guilt and stress build up, and productivity goes down. It is important to note that the guilt and stress are associated with the job itself. The employee does not understand that it is their task inertia causing the problem. Therefore, even holidays do little to aid productivity, and the only solution is to find a new job in which the context is reset and productivity can rise again.

Stress

Contrary to popular belief, unproductive people can be subject to a lot of stress. This is due to the guilt and stress cycle created by task inertia. When conditionally productive people are in an unproductive phase, their low productivity causes them to feel guilt because they know that they are capable of doing more and cannot understand why they are unable to work. They blame themselves, without understanding task inertia, and this guilt then causes stress. The stress then lowers productivity further, ensuring the cycle continues.

I know because I went through this cycle many times.

Guilt and stress cycles are one of the primary features of conditionally productive people.

At the new job, the employee finds a new lease on life. No longer burdened by guilt and stress, they suddenly find themselves free to work. They are also eager to make a good impression. This is important because it heightens the effect of any external management structures.

But time goes on, and the work becomes routine. Having impressed everyone, the employee unconsciously starts to relax. Tasks that they did without thinking before are now delayed until they are strictly necessary. Their productivity drops, which begins to cause guilt and stress. Stress causes task inertia to rise further, guaranteeing that the cycle can continue.

Improving productivity

Conditionally productive people will see the most benefit from reducing their task inertia. Not only will this directly increase their productivity, it will also lower their stress levels and increase job satisfaction. The next two chapters will provide a detailed treatment plan that will help you to manage and lower your task inertia.

Super Productive

I was briefly Super Productive. I quit my job, and cashed in my retirement savings to start up a video game company. I was the only person working full time on the game, although I employed a few contractors to produce art and sound assets. I was the lead programmer and lead game designer, as well as project manager.

I became a very boring person. All day, the only things I did were eat, sleep and write code. I worked 7 days a week, I worked in the evenings, I worked whenever I could. What's interesting to me, looking back now, is that I never felt stressed. I thoroughly enjoyed that part of my life. It remains the most enjoyable programming I've ever done, even if it was also the most pointless programming I've ever done in that the game was ultimately never finished.

I worked from home on my game for about 8 months, when a lack of funds forced me to find contract work to further development. Suddenly I was working an 8 hour day job and trying to work on the game at night, and my motivation dropped. Soon I lost passion for the project altogether.

That was my experience of being super productive - able to sustain a high level of productivity while not feeling much stress. But as we will see later, not feeling much stress is in fact atypical for super productive people.

In my discussions with super productive people, I've realised they are built a little differently to most of us. While I was super productive for a while, I remain conditionally productive. But some people can sustain high levels of productivity consistently, and it is important for us to understand how they do this.

We've already seen how ego investment in the task being performed is responsible for the high task inertia that conditionally productive people feel. Thus, what gives super productive people their edge is that they invest their ego in the outcome of a task and not the performance of the task.

In other words, whether the task is boring is not important to them. What is important is how the task fits into the context of their goals and aspirations. By focusing on the outcome of the task rather than the process of performing the task, super productive people tend to suffer from less task inertia.

This is not to say that super productive people do not have task inertia. Many a high ranking executive has an unmowed lawn or a lightbulb that needs changing. The difference is that these tasks, while possibly important to others, are not important to the goals of the super productive person, and thus their task inertia remains high.

Super productive people suffer from different forms of stress to conditionally productive people.

In later chapters, we will discuss mindsets and habits to lower your task inertia and raise your productivity, modelled along how super productive people already do it.

Productivity Drivers

The greatest strength that super productive people have is their ability to pick a goal and dedicate themselves towards it. They pursue it relentlessly, at the cost of everything else.

Because of this, they almost completely lack task inertia, at least in the context of their chosen goal. Their productivity then depends almost entirely upon motivation. The more motivated they are, the harder they work.

Whereas conditionally productive have difficulty getting their brains to do the work they want to do, super productive people suffer no such problems. Their brains almost never rebel and tell them to browse YouTube for inane entertainment.

This also means that most of them have difficulty understanding task inertia theory itself. In their view, if you have work that you are paid to do, you need to do it. Anything else is laziness at best. The very idea that you could have work that you need to do, and find yourself unable to concentrate on it, is entirely out of their range of experience.

Stress

Because they are so driven, you might say that super productive people have "zero chill". They are unable to switch off. They suffer from high stress levels, which is sometimes what drives their productivity in the first place. But these high levels of stress are frequently unsustainable over a career, sometimes leading to burnout and even a higher incidence of physical disease.

Their stress comes from two sources. The first is identifying strongly with their work and engaging with their work to such a high degree that emotional transference takes place. To them, it isn't "just a job". If there is a workplace problem, they are personally affected, even when the cause is outside of their control.

The second source of stress is meeting their own high expectations. They place themselves under a significant amount of pressure to perform as well as they believe they ought to, and this can make them tightly wound.

Improving productivity

Super productive people tend to be high achievers in the workplace. They rise fast and go far. Their problem is figuring out how to make this sustainable. They likely hate the phrase "work-life balance", considering it to be either nonsense, or a contradiction.

The challenge for them would be to avoid burnout in the long term, or even more severe consequences.

The End Goal – Directionally Productive

Should we all aspire to be super productive? No, I don't think so. Some, but not all, super productive people are so driven that they suffer from burnout. Some of them ignore stress instead of dealing with it, the result being that after a few years, they are simply unable to cope.

My ideal goal, and I hope yours too, is to be productive when I want to be productive, while not suffering from too much stress. My end goal is thus to be directionally productive –

productive at my own discretion, but able to rest and relax whenever I need to.

This book is primarily written to help conditionally productive people lower their task inertia enough that they can be directionally productive. If you are super productive and would like to relax a little in order to become directionally productive, I'm afraid that this book can be of little help. It may be oversimplifying things to state that this book is intended to help conditionally productive people become more productive, whereas super productive people would need to sacrifice a little productivity in order to lower their stress.

Chapter Summary

- Unmotivated people are almost completely unproductive and little affected by task inertia. Their problem is motivation, not task inertia.

- Conditionally productive people, which is most of us, have our productivity depend on both motivation and task inertia.

- Task inertia can cause guilt and stress cycles, further lowering productivity.

- Super productive have their productivity depend almost entirely on motivation. They suffer little if any task inertia.

- The goal is to become directionally productive - able to be productive at will, without the burden of high stress suffered by super productive people.

Chapter 4

Treatment plan for task inertia

Now that we understand task inertia, we can do something about it. Our treatment plan for task inertia takes a two-pronged approach - we will be correcting beliefs that serve to reinforce task inertia, and providing active steps for you to take that will help you to manage your task inertia.

You have already taken the first step towards managing your task inertia, which is understanding it. Previously, you did not know why it was difficult for you to work, and you blamed yourself for this. Now you know that the reality is more complex than this. This knowledge should help you begin correcting some of your beliefs and work habits. This chapter deals with faulty beliefs that may be making the symptoms of your task inertia more severe. Once you have read this chapter, and corrected any faulty beliefs you may have had, you will have made another important step on the road to recovery.

You can change your brain

As we have seen, high task inertia is caused by faulty beliefs and work habits. In order to correct these, we need to instil new beliefs and new habits. You may feel that your beliefs and habits that give rise to your task inertia are deeply ingrained. While this is true, it is important to rather focus on the possible growth that you can achieve, and how this could enable you to achieve the productivity you have always wanted.

We all have the potential for significant changes to the very deepest levels of our brains. We all have the potential for significant growth. Science has shown that our brains are more plastic and more capable of growth that we used to believe, and the fantastic thing is that this growth is within our control.

Simply put, your mind can change your brain for the better. All this requires is that you invest the time and effort. I learned exactly this from dealing with a highly personal situation, which I will share with you, because it is what taught me that we can change our brains with time.

I am a childhood trauma survivor. Amongst other things, I had to deal with the death of my father when I was 15, a mother with mental illness who alternated between being loving and abusive, and periods of relative poverty. My mother then died when I was 22, leaving me with no parents or grandparents.

I spent the next 8 years trying to recover. I saw a therapist for a long time. I meditated. I read books. But nothing seemed to help. I was still in so much pain, years after my mother had died. People said I should just get over it, and move on. The frustrating thing was, that was exactly what I was trying to do. But no matter what I did, it seemed to have relatively little impact on my quality of life. I still had bouts of depression nearly a decade after my mother had died.

One particularly bad weekend, I went for a walk, and during that walk I realised I was a childhood trauma survivor. I was 30 years old, and it was the first time I realised that I had been through childhood trauma. I got back home after my walk, and resolved to read all that I could about childhood trauma.

What I read was eye opening. It explained that childhood trauma has long term effects on the developing brain of a child, and hampers the ability of the child to cope with stressful situations as an adult. Simply put, the tap that releases stress hormones is opened all the way, and the child

71

cannot switch it off. This tap is open because the brain required those stress chemicals to cope with childhood. But the problem is that, as the child grows into an adult, they inherit the same faulty stress mechanisms which they are unable to switch off. This is why childhood trauma sufferers tend to suffer from higher stress levels as adults.

Discovering that this was why I had struggled so much as an adult set me free. I finally understood why I was suffering, and that made me able to endure the suffering. Even better, the book provided information on the emerging science of neuroplasticity, and how the science of changing and growing your brain over time can enable you to make major improvements in your quality of life (*). Neuroplasticity is highly relevant for improving task inertia related problems, but fortunately, not as intractable as problems caused by childhood trauma.

In a similar way to how understanding the effects of childhood trauma enabled me to better endure the resultant suffering, understanding task inertia has enabled me to lower my related stress due to low productivity. When I feel unproductive now, I understand the drivers of my low productivity. I understand the guilt and stress cycle that further lowers productivity. Even without making any further changes, this understanding dramatically improves my attitude towards myself and my productivity levels. I hope the same is true for you.

Even without changing working habits, the lower stress that results from understanding task inertia theory and how it applies to one's productivity can itself lead to higher productivity. Awareness of task inertia has some real benefits in this regard, and it is worth examining some beliefs that you may hold that may be worsening the effects of your task inertia.

Our treatment plan for task inertia is thus two-pronged. In this chapter, we will examine some beliefs that you may have, that can make the effects of task inertia worse. Reading and understanding this chapter will help you change your mind on some important topics, which may change how you approach your work. There are some exercises for you to do, which may help you internalise the advice.

In the next chapter, we will discuss the treatment plan itself, which is a step by step process that will help you reform your working habits and become as productive as you have ever wanted to be. This treatment plan takes time, because it involves changing how your brain works and how you see work. However, the results will be worth it.

General advice for coping with task inertia

Before we get into the treatment plan, we'll cover some general advice which will be useful to keep in mind as you go on. These are things you should be aware of. It may be that some of your beliefs around work and productivity may need adjusting in order to minimize the effects of your task inertia. To help you get there, read the following passages and then complete the exercises that follow.

Don't make decisions based on task inertia

I have spent much of my working career searching for that one job or that one career that would inspire me to work hard. I was hoping that I'd come across a job advert bathed in a heavenly beam of light, a clear sign that I should apply and that this job would be the end of my woes.

I couldn't understand how people like Bill Gates and Elon Musk seemed to have no doubts as to what inspired them, and indeed, many of my colleagues seemed to know exactly where they wanted to go and how they wanted to get there.

I felt lost. I was only inconsistently productive, and I felt that I lacked direction. A lot of the changes in career direction that I initiated over my life were a search for that one inspirational job that would unlock my productivity and make me happy.

For instance, I changed jobs in order to move to a job that I believed required more interrupt mode work than concentration mode work. This worked great, until it didn't. All professional level jobs require concentration mode some of the time, and so, by trying to move to a job that required less concentration mode work, I'd created a situation where the quality of my work in interrupt mode tasks greatly exceeded the quality of my work in concentration mode tasks. In other words, I merely shifted the problem around, without solving it.

After discovering task inertia theory, I realised that there are a few problems with this approach. Moving because of task inertia is a bad idea, for reasons that I've mentioned above. If you're searching for a job that will pull the productivity out of you, you won't find it. You have to create the productivity yourself. It isn't easy, especially if you have had bad habits for a long time, but it is possible.

Your employer is responsible for creating an environment in which you can succeed. You are responsible for performing your best within that environment. Your employer is responsible for perhaps 50% of your productivity. You are responsible for the rest. You have to make the choice to do your work as best you can. The party that will benefit the most from high productivity is actually you.

I don't mean that you need to work long hours or sacrifice your free time in order to be productive. I mean that in the time allocated to your work, you should aim to be as productive as possible.

All of which you have no doubt heard before. But if you have been searching for the right job where you will feel motivated to give your best, then perhaps it would be better to rephrase that as you will search for the right job where you will choose to give your best. Make productivity as something you choose to provide, not something that your employer pulls out of you.

Exercise

Have you made any decisions based on task inertia? Think carefully about how task inertia has influenced your decision making over your professional life. I'd encourage you to either write this down or tell a friend that you can trust. Communicating our thoughts into a medium that can be understood by others is a powerful way of organising them.

Don't overemphasize inspiration

Our culture prizes inspiration as the source of motivation that drives high productivity and success, and I think we overvalue it. You can see this in software engineer adverts - most of them value software engineers who will write code in their spare time. The implication is that you should love programming so much that you do it in your free time even when you are not being paid to do so.

By placing the emphasis on inspiration, you risk creating a situation in which you will never be truly productive because you will never feel that inspiration you so crave. A few of us lucky mortals are the Elon Musks, Bill Gates and Stephen Kings of this world, who know exactly what we want and go out and get it. The rest of us just want to feel happy in our jobs.

The problem is that this emphasis on inspiration creates expectations in our heads that are impossible to reach. Worse, it biases our decision making towards the irrational, because who knows what work will inspire you?

Inspiration is a good thing - if you have it. If not, then just do the best you can at your work place. Stop putting these expectations on yourself that you need to find your inspiration in order to be truly fulfilled and productive. You just need a job that pays the bills with colleagues that you get on with and work that you find interesting.

Make a choice

In the midst of the COVID-19 pandemic, I realised that it was time to abandon my search for an inspiring job or even an inspiring career. Throughout my life, I had been hoping for a gut feel that would tell me what to do. I thought one's career direction ought to be dictated by what one enjoys doing. I thought I should "follow my inspiration" - but I didn't have any.

The problem with this is that it was mostly a search for lower task inertia. Had I discovered a magical job in which I had low task inertia on a permanent basis, I think I would have been happy. But unfortunately, that is a fantasy because task inertia is solely in our own control, not the control of our employer.

The second problem with such a search of course is that not everyone is inspired, and that is okay. At the age of 35, if I wasn't already inspired, it is likely that I never will be. That doesn't mean that I'm a poor employee or unproductive, it simply means that I have to choose what I do rather than "follow my passions."

I needed something to replace my search for inspiration, and I realised that the answer was simple - choice. If I choose to do something, even if it doesn't inspire me, then I can take responsibility for my decisions. I can take responsibility for my productivity or lack thereof in this role, and this is actually a very important step in overcoming task inertia.

One of the reasons task inertia arises is because we externalise our conditions for productivity. We say to ourselves that we will be productive when we have a deadline, or we will be productive when the boss is looking over our shoulder. This also means that we are externalising control and responsibility, as we are no longer in control of when we are productive - that now depends upon external factors. Productivity is thus not a dial that we can turn up when we want to get things done - productivity is something that happens in response to external stimuli.

By now, you can see the harm this causes in your own life. If your productivity depends upon external factors, this can be very frustrating for you if you just want to get a bit of work done. The only solution is to internalise your control over your productivity, so that it makes no difference whether you have a deadline coming up or a boss looking over your shoulder.

The first step in internalising control over your productivity is to realise that you have been externalising it and that this is unhealthy. The second step is to make sure that you make choices regarding the work you do.

When you choose to do something, even if it is not something for which you feel inspiration, you can take responsibility for that choice, and this allows you to start taking control of your productivity back. You stop being a passive observer, watching your productivity levels go up and down, and instead become an active worker.

Exercise

Inspiration vs choice - which applies to you better? Are you driven by inspiration? If you are, what inspires you? Write it down or communicate it to a friend.

If you aren't driven by inspiration, that's okay too. Many people are not. But you still have to make a choice. What choice will you make? You don't need to decide right this second, but you need to accept that the choice is yours to make, and yours alone. Write down a few options available to you, and evaluate each of them in terms of how well they suit you.

Take responsibility for your productivity

Some of the factors that influence task inertia are external in nature. We have discussed examples such as deadlines or other pressure. It is important to note that when these external factors are the dominant factors in your productivity, you will be at a risk of experiencing task inertia. This is because your productivity is no longer something you control, but something which is heavily influenced by external factors. This can lead to a feeling of powerlessness, as well as the guilt and stress cycle which we have already discussed.

Therefore, we need to move from external control to internal control. We need to become self-directed in our work. This is called regaining agency. The way to do this is to take responsibility for your productivity.

So what does taking responsibility mean in this context? It means acknowledging that you are not a passive observer in your working life, and are responsible for your productivity, as well as what you choose to be productive in.

Some of the exercises above, such as making choices, are part of taking responsibility. It is important that you exercise your choice in every facet of your working life. Don't be a passive observer, make choices and head in a direction of your choosing.

The counterpoint to this is of course guilt.

Should you feel guilt when your task inertia comes up and you find yourself unable to work? Guilt is a natural impulse. We feel obligations to others, and want to fulfil those obligations. You feel an obligation to your company, not because they pay you but because you are loyal to them. You feel an obligation towards your boss, because you like them and don't want to disappoint them.

Therefore, the first thing I want to be clear about, is don't beat yourself up for feeling guilty. Like a lot of negative emotions, guilt can easily cause spirals, where your guilt leads you to doubting yourself, being harder on yourself. Consequently, your level of confidence declines, and you may disengage further. So, don't worry if you feel guilty.

But what you should recognise is that guilt serves little purpose here. It isn't an emotion that leads to productivity - instead, it tends to be paralysing. Your company or your boss do not need your guilt, they need your output. Your energy would be better spent uncovering the reasons why you are having strong task inertia at the moment, so that you can correct it, than feeling guilty for not working.

Exercise

Do you take responsibility for your productivity? Or is it largely influenced by external factors? Think about this, and write down how you feel, or communicate it to a friend. It is important that you become aware of the factors that influence your productivity, and how much control you have over them.

Do you feel guilty when you are not productive? How guilty do you feel? Is it a paralysing guilt? Think about any guilt you feel, and the reasons for it.

How would you judge a colleague who struggled with productivity like you do? Would you judge them harshly or be more understanding? Write down what you would think, or communicate it to a friend. Is this different to how you view yourself?

Chapter Summary

- You can rewire your brain to learn new working habits that work for you. It just takes time.

- Don't make decisions based on task inertia.

- Don't overemphasize inspiration.

- Take responsibility for your productivity, but don't overdo it on the guilt.

References

* - Fuchs, Eberhard & Flugge, Gabriele. (2014). *Adult Neuroplasticity: More Than 40 Years of Research. Neural plasticity.* 2014. 541870. 10.1155/2014/541870.

Chapter 5
Managing task inertia

Take an evaluation

Before you go any further, you should take some time to explore what the root cause of your current productivity problems are. You may identify with what I have written about task inertia, and you may believe that you suffer from task inertia. All the same, it is worth exploring the root cause of your productivity woes in more detail, because there could be other causes, such as low motivation.

It is possible for you to just not be motivated in your current role. Remember that, even if you were motivated before, you might not be motivated any longer. Your motivation levels can change for a variety of reasons, including boredom and lack of challenge. In fact, high task inertia can itself cause a lack of motivation, as it can cause a great deal of frustration and stress, feelings that you may transfer onto the role itself.

Bear in mind that you could have a general pattern of task inertia as well as low motivation for your current role. If that is the case, then both issues will need to be tackled in order for your productivity to improve and your stress to lower back down. Motivation and task inertia are linked, and can affect each other. Therefore, any treatment plan will need to take both into account.

You also need to think about which parts of your life suffer from low productivity the most. I'm going to split these into two broad categories. The first is employment related productivity problems, which apply to any situation in which you are expected to work in exchange for money and are not running your own business. The second is entrepreneurial productivity problems, which apply to any project or business that you are working on in your own time. This applies even if you have not "made it" yet and are still permanently employed.

Educational situations can be a little strange. They can blur the lines between employment situations and entrepreneurial situations, because while you may have a lecturer, teacher or facilitator, they do not direct or plan your work.

The better you understand your current situation, the more effective you will be at improving it. To help you with this,

I've written a questionnaire which will help you to identify the cause of your current productivity problems. When you answer it, keep in mind the productivity situation that you are concerned about, whether that be employment related or entrepreneurial related. If you like, you can take the questionnaire more than once, for each situation that interests you.

Productivity questionnaire

1. In the last 6 months, how often have you worked late for any reason?

Never (1)   Infrequently (2)   Sometimes (3)
      Often (4)   Very often (5)

2. It is 6PM on a Friday and you've finished work for the week. A colleague sends you a message and asks for help with something. They say it is urgent but will only take a few minutes. It isn't your responsibility, but you have context of the situation. How likely are you to help?

Never (1)   Infrequently (2)   Sometimes (3)
      Often (4)   Very often (5

3. How much do you identify with your company's vision and mission? How excited are you to be working for your company?

Not at all (1)   Not very (2)   Uncertain (3)   A   little   (4)
　　A lot (5)

4. How do you feel about the tasks that you do in your role? Do you enjoy your work?

Not at all (1)   Not very (2)   Uncertain (3)   A   little   (4)
　　A lot (5)

5. Do you enjoy the tasks that you do less, even though the tasks themselves have not changed? How much has your enjoyment of your tasks changed over the last 6 months?

Enjoyment increased (1)   No change (2)   Slight decrease (3)   Large decrease (4)   Major decrease (5)

6. In the last 6 months, how frequently have you felt frustrated with yourself for not getting work done?

Never (1)   Infrequently (2)   Sometimes (3)
　　Often (4)   Very often (5)

7. In the last 6 months, how frequently have you gone more than an hour without working, when you know you should be? In other words, how frequently have you not been able to concentrate on work for more than an hour during the middle of the working day?

Never (1)   Infrequently (2)   Sometimes (3)
        Often (4)   Very often (5)

8. In the last 6 months, how frequently have you felt guilty for the amount of work that you get done in a day? I'm specifically referring to moments when you did little, got away with it, and felt guilty about it?

Never (1)   Infrequently (2)   Sometimes (3)
        Often (4)   Very often (5)

Interpreting your results

Now that you have completed the questionnaire, you can calculate your results and get a better picture of what is driving your productivity problems.

Questions 1 through 4 relate to motivation. Add up the numbers in brackets next to each answer that you selected, and compare that number to the table below:

1-6	Completely unmotivated
7-12	Relatively Unmotivated
13-16	Motivated
17-20	Highly motivated

Questions 5 through 8 relate to task inertia. Add up the numbers in brackets next to each answer that you selected, and compare that number to the table below:

1-4	No task inertia
5-10	Low task inertia
11-15	Moderate task inertia
16-20	High task inertia

Deciding on a course of action

This book will be of most benefit to you if you're suffering from moderate to high task inertia. I suffered from high task inertia, and following the actions and strategies in this book helped me become far more productive. You can change your brain and improve your working habits - it just takes time.

If you suffer from no to low task inertia, this book may still help boost your productivity by teaching you about goals, targets, habits and evaluation. These are handy strategies for anyone wishing to improve their productivity, so they may still benefit you.

What if you have low motivation?

What should you do if you have both low motivation and high task inertia?

First you need to understand that while they are separate drivers of productivity, they do influence each other. If you have high task inertia, and you struggle to be productive, this can lower your motivation. You might feel disheartened and lacking in confidence owing to your difficulty in performing work, and your perceived lower productivity can cause your stress to spike.

But there is still hope. I'd suggest working through this book, because you might be able to get your motivation back on track by getting your task inertia under control. At the very least, the fact that you are taking positive action towards improving yourself and your working habits might make you feel good about yourself and optimistic for the future. This could lower your stress, and cause your motivation to rise again.

Don't lose hope. The world can look quite dark when you are unmotivated and highly stressed, but if you persevere, you can improve yourself, your productivity, and your life.

The management plan

In the previous chapter, we discussed mindset changes that are helpful for lowering task inertia. Changing how you see your tasks, job and career can have a profound impact on not only your task inertia but also your entire career trajectory. You may have held these beliefs that weren't serving you for years, and now that you have changed your mind, you might be able to start making decisions that benefit you.

But the brain is a stubborn thing. You understand task inertia now, but your brain still falls into the same trap very easily. In order for you to improve your working habits, you will have to invest some time every day for the next few months. This is how long it will take for your brain to adopt the new program that we want it to have.

It may be that you will need to reread this book from time to time, whenever you are struggling, to remind yourself what you ought to be doing to minimize task inertia. That's okay. The steps in this book will help you get back on track, whenever you feel that you aren't productive and are frustrated because of this.

The management plan for task inertia involves 3 things - habits, targets, and evaluation. All three of these elements work together synergistically, and so working on all three tends to produce better results. But don't think you need to go from where you are - struggling to work and feeling bad about yourself - to mastering habits, targets and evaluation in a single day. If you can work on your habits for the first week, or even the first month, that's fine. You can always reread this book and then start working on the next element.

You proceed at your own pace. There is no single pace that I can recommend that will work for everyone. What is more important is that you understand what is involved and why it is needed. Remember what we talked about in the previous chapter - you need to take responsibility for your productivity. That includes taking responsibility for improving it. Therefore, you control the pace at which you work on improving your productivity.

The way that these elements interact is that habits are what keep you working every day, targets are what you are working towards, and evaluation keeps you on track. We'll talk more about each element in their respective section.

In short, your daily habits are a key mechanism for lowering the task inertia of the tasks you work on. This is because repetition helps to build neural pathways that take your ego out of the equation when it comes to deciding whether to do a task. You become so habituated to it, that you don't need to think about whether to do the task, you only think about the task itself.

Target setting is a key mechanism for recovering your productivity. At first you will be setting tiny targets that are easy to accomplish but have meaning in the wider context. This is the key to building up momentum and retraining your brain.

Lastly, evaluation keeps you on track. A habit with nothing to reinforce it will likely eventually wane, and so evaluation will help ensure that you stick to your habits over the long term.

But first, we need to talk about awareness.

Be aware of your task inertia

The previous chapter covered some philosophy that you should be aware of, to help you change your thought patterns. These altered thought patterns will be helpful to reduce the impact of task inertia, as you will see that some of your previous thought patterns may not have been helpful.

While this is a solid start and on its own can result in a sizable reduction in task inertia, there is more work to do.

Your brain develops neural pathways which encode commonly used habits and ways of thinking. If you are an adult now and have had task inertia for some time, it is likely that your habits and ways of thinking are deeply ingrained. Think of them like short circuits. These short circuits are highly optimized to make your brain as efficient as possible. So much so, that you don't even notice you are using them. Sometimes, the thought that a task is boring or not essential will not even come to your conscious mind. You will simply feel resistance to performing the task.

Because of the deeply ingrained nature of these short circuits, changing them takes time and effort. This is why becoming more productive is not a simple matter of willpower. Lacking productivity doesn't mean you don't "want it" badly enough. Lacking productivity doesn't mean you are "lazy". It just means you have task inertia.

You understand task inertia now, which gives you insight into the inner workings of your brain when you are struggling to be productive. You now need to use that understanding to change your habits and thought patterns.

The way to do this is by labelling any resistance to perform work as task inertia. Over time, this will lessen your task inertia and make it more manageable.

In more detail, throughout a working day, your brain will want to use the short circuit that forms your task inertia many times. If you're under pressure to get work done, it may use the short circuit less. If there is less pressure at work, you will use it more.

Every time you feel task inertia, you know that your brain is trying to use the short circuit. This is where your conscious mind needs to step in and label that thought as task inertia.

Even if you don't end up working, labelling your thought patterns as task inertia will bring it more under your conscious control. This is because you are externalising the difficulty you are having working. You realise that it is not because you are lazy, it is because your task inertia reared its ugly head. It isn't a part of your personality, it is simply a defective subroutine that we can correct. Later on, you will be able to form new ways of thinking about work that don't come with as much task inertia, and enable you to be more productive.

But the first step is to recognize and label your task inertia, and this needs to be done many times per day so that it becomes automatic. Any time you feel mental resistance to performing a task, you need to label it as task inertia.

This sounds like it is philosophy, and you may think it belongs in the previous section. But it really isn't. This is something you have to do actively with your mind. You have to train yourself to label your difficulty in performing your work as task inertia, and stop blaming yourself for it.

Exercise

Every day, take 5 minutes out of your day to think about whether you struggled with task inertia today. If you did, don't judge yourself. Just note the simple fact that you struggled with it. What was going through your head at the time? What did you do instead of working?

Chapter Summary

- Take the Employment Productivity Questionnaire and learn how to interpret your results.

- The management plan will focus on goals, targets, habits and evaluation.

- Be aware of your task inertia - practice awareness every day.

Chapter 6

Goals and Targets

Target setting is an important part of goal directed behaviour. As we've covered previously, thinking in terms of goals helps us think of tasks in terms of their value to our goals rather than how we feel about the task. It takes our ego out the equation and lets us see the task for what it is - something that needs doing that we should avoid attaching too much personal feeling to.

Goal setting also forces us to make choices about what we want to achieve and why we want to achieve these things. If we're making choices, then we're taking control over our actions, and this is an extremely important step towards internalising control over our productivity.

Super productive people do this - they work in the context of their goals, rather than how tasks make them feel. Thus, one of the important parts of becoming more productive is identifying your goals.

Goal setting

Your goals help you define where you are going. They help you keep your eyes on the horizon, instead of getting mired in your current situation.

Simply put, a goal is a result you want to achieve. The specific types of goals that we are interested in as far as reducing task inertia goes are those goals that have a time horizon of about 1-3 years, and represent something that is within your capability to achieve.

The goal you choose should be personal to you. It could be related to your permanent employment, or it could be a side venture. What is important is that the goal represent something you want to achieve.

If you're experiencing high task inertia at your work place, then it makes sense to choose a workplace related goal. It makes no sense to work on a side project hoping that this will reduce your task inertia at your primary job.

Thus, if you're experiencing high task inertia at your primary job, create a goal for yourself that relates to that. It could be something like finish a particular project on time or land an important client. I'd advise you to avoid selecting getting a promotion or an award as a goal, as these are often not within our control, even if we work hard.

SMART Goals

You may have heard of the acronym SMART, which represents Specific, Measurable, Achievable, Relevant and Tangible. These are all said to be good qualities for goals to possess, but as we'll see, not all of them are necessary for productivity goals.

Specific

Specific refers to a goal having a defined outcome, or relating to a specific person or project. Having specific goals means that you understand exactly what you are trying to do.

Measurable

Measurable means that it should be possible to measure how close you are to completion of the goal. An example might be writing an 80000 word book - it is easy to count how many words you have written, and you can use this to track your progress. However, experienced writers know that a book is not done when your word count hits 80000 - it is done when you believe it is done, which may involve several rounds of editing. Thus, while having measurable goals is a good idea, I don't think it is necessary for productivity.

Achievable

Your goal should be something attainable that encourages you to push a little. This means it should be something that you can realistically achieve within the timeframe that you set out. It also means that it must be within your control. I've already used the example of a promotion - the problem with having a promotion as your goal is that, in most cases, it is out of your control, but dependent upon a space opening up and you being selected for the role.

Relevant

Your goal needs to be relevant to you, and relevant to the specific area where you want to grow. It needs to align with your other goals, and where you are going in life. An example might be that you are suffering from terrible task inertia in your primary employment, and this is causing you much guilt and stress. Your goal then should relate to your primary place of employment and not to a side project. Unfortunately, it will do you little good to work on a side project hoping that this will make you more productive in your day job. In order to boost productivity in your day job, you need a goal that relates to your day job.

You might then have multiple goals. At least one to boost productivity in your day job, and then as many as are necessary for your side projects, if any.

Time bound

Your goal should have a target date for you to work towards. This will keep create a little internal pressure in your mind to get things moving. In the case of a side project, it can be whatever you want, but preferably not more than two years away. In the case of your primary employment, I suggest aligning this to your deliverables at work. If your deliverables are too frequent, I'd suggest a recurring goal. However, take care not to align your goals with your sprints, if you work in sprints. Sprints are typically two weeks in length, and this is too short for a goal to have much impact. I'd suggest a longer time horizon, such as 6 months.

If you work in an environment with frequent deliverables, I'd suggest creating a goal with a 6 month target date that focuses on the quality of your output in that time, as well as meeting all requirements. We'll get into target setting below, but this might break down into targets of updating the status of any tickets you are working on once per day, and always completing at least one ticket per day.

Some other definitions of SMART goals substitute Tangible for T, instead of time bound. I prefer time bound, because not all worthwhile goals are tangible. This is related to measurable above, in fact. If you have to pick one of the two properties for your goal to have, a time bound task is likely to motivate you more than a necessarily tangible goal will.

Exercise

Create some goals now. What do you want to achieve? When do you want to achieve it by?

Lastly, write what the accomplishment of the goal will mean to you. How will you feel?

Target setting

With your goals created, you need to create daily or weekly targets that will connect your day to day activities to the goal in question. These targets are necessary to focus your attention onto what needs doing.

By setting targets that move us towards our goals, we light the path that shows us what we need to do. This is an important part of keeping your eyes on the horizon, and to keep your ego from getting too involved in the tasks that you do.

In order to set targets, you must be able to break your goal into small achievable pieces of work. This way you will be able to say whether you hit your target or not. The sum total of these small targets, over a long enough period of time, should result in the achievement of the goal. At the very least, each time you meet your targets, you should be a little closer to your goal.

A good example of this is, if you were writing a book, to set an approximate word count that you would like to meet by a certain date as your goal. Perhaps you would like to have written 80000 words in 12 months time. If you write at a pace of 300 words per day, you will have written 80000 words by day 267, with some days to spare for editing and for the inevitable duvet days.

Each time you write 300 words in a day, you know that you are moving closer to your goal at a pace that will result in the achievement of this goal by the date that you have set.

But what if your goal is not related to a project like writing a book, but instead related to being productive at work? That may be a little more difficult to measure than whether a book is completed, but nonetheless, you can still use it to improve your productivity as long as you create appropriate targets that connect your daily work to your goal.

So suppose that your goal is to raise your productivity level at work. Perhaps your work is divided into two week sprints, and you are assigned tasks to complete in the two weeks. A target to complete all of your work by the end of the sprint is not likely to be effective because it does not relate to daily activity. Your brain might choose to procrastinate in the hopes that you can get all of your work done in the last 2 days. Even if you could do this, this causes unnecessary stress on yourself, and means that stakeholders who depend on your work get the completed work later than they need to.

Therefore, you should divide up your tasks for the sprint and assign yourself targets to complete at least one task each day. You should break the tasks down as much as you need to, in order to ensure that you have a unit of work that can be completed inside a single day.

We'll go through the general process of target setting and then go over some helpful tips to make your targets work better for you.

How to set targets

The characteristics of goals that we discussed above - namely Specific, Measurable, Achievable, Relevant and Time-bound - should be used to guide the creation of your targets. We'll go over these characteristics below, in their order of importance to target setting.

Relevant

The most important of these characteristics is the relevance of the target to the goal. Make sure that, if you achieve your daily or weekly targets that relate to this goal, that the goal itself will be achieved. For instance, if the goal is to write a book, the target should relate to writing a certain number of words per day. If your goal is weight loss, your targets may relate to healthy food eaten or distance walked.

It is important to realise that your targets may change as your progress with your goal. For instance, as you progress with writing your book, you may have to switch from writing to marketing, and so perhaps your targets will change when that happens. This is part of the importance of a regular evaluation cycle, discussed in a later chapter.

Time-bound and Measurable

With your goal created and a due date set, you can work backwards to find out what you need to do every day in order to achieve your goal. The Time-bound and Measurable characteristics relate to each other in that a shorter time duration requires more work to be done every day.

If your task is measurable, it will thus be easier to calculate how much work needs to be done every day or every week, by dividing up the work. If your task is not measurable, it will be more difficult to ensure that you are on track to complete the task. This might also be the case for work that is measurable, but where the measurement is uncertain. An example would be teaching yourself a new skill such as a programming language. If you are new to programming, you might not know how long it will take to master the language. Therefore, while you will make progress, your progress will be difficult to measure.

If your task is not easily measurable, then regular evaluation of your progress becomes even more important. You can gain a better idea of how you are progressing by taking some time to evaluate your progress every week.

Achievable

Ensure that you can realistically achieve the target that you would be setting every day. Once you know how much work must be done every day, you may wish to adjust the due date for the task, if the amount of work required every day or every week is not feasible for you. It is better to be realistic with what you can achieve, especially if you are suffering from productivity problems, than set an overly ambitious goal and possibly set yourself up for failure. There is another reason for choosing smaller targets, which we will get into below.

Some target setting advice

Below you'll find some advice for target setting which applies if you are suffering from task inertia. If you're unproductive and want to change that, read on. If you are already somewhat productive, then the below advice may not help you as much.

Set small targets

If you're starting from a place of low productivity, it will be better for you if you set your targets to be small, rather than large. It is more important to work consistently every day, even if only in small amounts, than to aim for a massive effort in one day.

I hadn't written in a long time. I kept putting it off. I didn't know it at the time, but this was because the task inertia for writing was just too high. I stumbled upon habits before I had discovered task inertia. I decided that I needed to try to form a writing habit, and that I needed a word target to ensure that I wrote every day.

I picked 200 words as my daily word target. I can write 200 words in 15 minutes. It is one tenth or less of what more practiced novelists can do in a day. But there were good reasons why I picked such a low word count, and why you should also set low targets when recovering from high task inertia.

The biggest risk to our productivity over time is not those days where we worked 6 hours instead of 8, but the days where we worked 0 hours rather than 2. Setting low targets help ensure that you actually work every day, which is important for two reasons.

The first is that prior to this, you were making no progress at all. Even 15 minutes per day starts to add up quickly, and in a few weeks, you will be amazed at how far you have come. That progress will make you feel better about yourself.

The second reason is that while you are working at the task, you are also working on your working habits. This is what we talked about in the previous section. You are training your brain to be more effective at work.

How high or how low you set your work targets should depend upon how productive you are now. If you are slightly productive but would like to become more productive, then set your targets a little higher than where you are now. If you are not productive at all, like I wasn't, then set your targets as small as possible until you have built the habit. Building a habit takes a few weeks, and if all goes well, you might feel the inclination to increase your daily targets.

Every day that you hit your small targets is thus a good day. Not only have you done work, but you are also retraining your working habits. You are changing those neural connections which govern how you relate to work. Over time, you can build up your targets once you have rebuilt your working habits. This will allow you to get more done.

Exercise

Now that you have created your goals, you can create some targets that will help you achieve these goals. Remember to cut yourself some slack in the pace, especially at first. Make sure that your targets are relevant to how productive you can be right now.

Chapter Summary

- Goals help keep your eyes on the horizon, instead of mired in your current situation.

- Goal setting involves making choices about where you want to go.

- Target setting helps you take responsibility for accomplishing your goal.

- Set small targets to keep work moving.

Chapter 7 -

Habits

   Goals and targets provide the what and the why that directs your daily work. Habits provide the how, and are an essential piece of keeping you on track and productive.

Habits are any activity performed with a regular routine. This might include something as mundane as brushing your teeth, or something more exciting such as working on that novel first thing in the morning. For our purposes, we will be looking at the kinds of habits that relate to increasing your productivity.

Habits are a powerful means of becoming more productive, and much as been written about them. But until now, I didn't understand why habits were effective at increasing productivity. The reason is simple - when you perform a habit often enough, you stop thinking about whether you should do it, and instead, you think about the task itself. When the habit becomes ingrained, your ego is not so active in deciding whether it wants to do the task, and so the task gets done. The decision of whether to do the task or not gets suborned to the reason why you have the habit in the first place, which is to meet your targets and thus your goals.

Over time, habits allow you to bring a bit more intention to the work that you do, and this will help you internalise control over your own productivity.

Therefore, building new habits is a powerful way of addressing task inertia, especially when combined with target and goal setting. Target and goal setting drive what you do every day and every week, while habits provide the structure for getting work done.

We'll cover some of the basics of what makes an effective habit, and what you can do to get more out of your habits.

Like goals, there are a few basic criteria that habits should possess, and most of these should be no surprise to you by now.

Relevant

The most important criteria for a productivity habit that you want to establish is that it is relevant to the goal and target that you're working with. If it isn't, nothing else matters. Your habit has to move you a little bit closer to the goal that you want to achieve.

Remember that you're not going to be able to complete your goal in one marathon session. Or two marathon sessions. If you could, your goal was too small to begin with. You're going to need to work on your goal for a few months at least. For this reason, your habit needs to get you a little bit closer to your goal.

What is relevant to the goal will probably change as you progress with the goal. This is why you should spend some time evaluating your progress every week - you'll identify when the work you need to do changes.

Regular

The next most important criteria of a habit is that you perform it on a regular basis. Not only because this is how you will make progress towards your goal, but also because it is important in helping you change the neural pathways in your brain that make it easier for you to work in the first place. We'll get into this in more detail below, but for now, just realise that keeping a habit is its own reward, in addition to the work you do during it.

You can schedule your habits according to time, or associate them with some activity. They can be weekly, or daily, or only on working days. It depends on what suits you and what will help you meet your targets and goals.

My weekly habit is to have an evaluation session with myself on Sunday evening at 6PM. I like winding down and having a quiet Sunday evening before the week of work, and a weekly check-in before the week begins helps me prepare for the week ahead, and keep me focused on my goals.

My daily habit is to write every morning, first thing in the morning. Actually, the first thing I do is to write a to-do list for the day, which we'll get into below. I don't write according to a set time schedule, I write until I'm done whatever I'm writing with. But in the past, I've used word targets.

When I lived in Johannesburg, I used to take taxis to work, and I'd write while in the taxi. I would go into the office about 3 times per week, and each of those days, I'd spend about 45 minutes writing in the car. Luckily I don't suffer from motion sickness. Ironically, I got more writing done on days that I went into the office than on days that I didn't, even though I had more free time when I didn't go into the office. This was before I was aware of task inertia. So I had the motivation to write every day while in the car, but my work habits meant that I didn't write when not in a car.

Advice for maintaining effective habits

Write daily to-do lists

I recommend that you write a daily to-do list containing the tasks which have any task inertia. Sometimes this could include cleaning the house or mowing the lawn, or it could include cooking a big dinner. It all depends on what you find tends to create task inertia for you.

Of course, the most common tasks that this list would contain would be work related, since that tends to be the area where people experience the highest task inertia. Naturally, this means that your to-do list should contain mostly work related items.

There are two major benefits of daily to-do lists. The first is that it helps create internal accountability. In the absence of someone who will tell you what to do every day, you need to create your own accountability. To-do lists are a great way of doing that, as once you can see the task written down, you'll feel the desire to accomplish that task by the end of the day.

Accountability then is further reinforced the next day, when you look at the previous day's list and tick off what you achieved and cross off what you did not. Having a lot of crosses and few ticks on your page is not likely to make you feel good, and it is likely to make you want to tick off those tasks today.

The other benefit is that it makes you think about what you want to do in the first place. Sometimes, when our task inertia causes high stress, we want to disengage from work, and not even look at our tasks. Creating a to-do list forces you to engage with your work and identify things that need to be done. Just being aware of what you need to do means you are one step closer to actually doing the work.

When I write to-do lists, I like using a simple A5 ring bound notebook and pen. Although I am a computer scientist and thus am familiar with the wide range of apps available that can do the same thing, I like using pen and paper for to-do lists. This is because it gives them physical form. I can see my list without turning my computer on. If I move from one device to another, I don't have to migrate my to-do list over. When I tried keeping a to-do list on my computer, I found that I had the tendency to want to use the same file and update it. This didn't work, because it is easy for tasks to stay on your to-do list for days if not weeks. Using pen and paper means that if I don't do a task, I have to copy it over to the next day or explain to myself why it is no longer relevant. That tends to keep the to-do list from growing.

Of course, you can use whatever medium you prefer - even electronic. As long as it works for you and fits in with your life. I keep two to-do lists - one for personal things and one for work things.

One other thing you can do is list your goals as headings on your to-do list, and then list the relevant targets underneath your goals. This is a good way of connecting the habit to the target and then to the goal. It will remind you why you have chosen to engage in a particular habit.

Example

Here is an example to-do list which may be helpful for you. I want to stress that this is an example, and that you can structure your list in a way that makes sense for you. I write to-do lists, even on a Saturday, but you don't have to.

You can be as detailed as you like. Since this is something I do every day, I tend not to be too descriptive in my tasks. The list is only for me, after all.

But I do tend to write up a mix of both work related and non work related goals. This is mostly out of the feeling that it gives me - I feel good when I tick something off, even if that something is enjoyable for me, like catching up with friends.

Notice how I have used the goals or categories as headings, and then listed tasks or targets underneath them. This helps connect me to why I am doing the task in the first place, which tends to limit task inertia because I'm thinking of the importance of the task to my future rather than the task itself.

Dedicate your to-do list to someone else

As we saw in an earlier chapter, much of task inertia occurs because we invest our egos in the performance of a task rather than the outcome. We involve our own egos in the performance of this task, and so we tend to put off tasks that we deem as boring or too easy.

Unfortunately, as we know, this is not a winning strategy. Even the most perfect job has boring tasks that simply must be completed. There is no Goldilocks job full of tasks that are challenging but not too challenging. It simply doesn't exist, and chasing such a job tends to cause misery and career instability.

How do we then uninvest our ego from the performance of the task and invest it in the outcome of the task? One way of doing this it to think about the tasks's relevance to other people or even the organisation at large.

121

This can be done with your daily to-do list. For each task that you write down, write down who this task is relevant to. Dedicate the task to them. This person doesn't have to be aware that you are doing this - it is mostly to trick your mind into thinking about the task in relation to this other person rather than yourself.

Every single task that we do at work has stakeholders - sometimes these are our colleagues, but they can also be customers, partners or even the market at large. Therefore, no matter what task you are doing, you should be able to dedicate the task to the stakeholder to which it is relevant.

Keep the person in mind when you think about attempting the task. Once again, we need to change the way that we think about tasks with high task inertia, and so writing someone's name down on a list does little if we don't actively think about them while performing the task.

Example

> *Monday 2020-05-18*
>
> *Boss*
>
> Check my Jira tickets and make sure they are up to date
>
> *Sally at Tech Trading Platform*
>
> Prepare roadmap presentation
>
> *Sam from Major Bank*
>
> Create requirement ticket from meeting notes
>
> *Fitness*
>
> *Walk*
>
> Tabata
>
> *Writing*
>
> Write 200 words on task inertia

Here the headings I have used for the items on the list are a mixture of people that I am accountable to and personal goals that I want to achieve.

Add mastery to your boring tasks

From time to time, all of us will have to perform tasks that we find boring or uninteresting. You can't change this, but what you can change is the manner in which you perform those tasks, to make them more interesting.

You might aim to complete your tasks as quickly as possible – as long as you do not compromise the quality of your work. Or, you may aim to be extremely consistent and dependable with your administrative tasks.

Repetition is one of the key factors in building mastery, so, if there are boring tasks that must be done again and again, you might as well aim to master them. Aiming to master the task then becomes the goal, rather than the performance of the task itself – transferring your ego investment from the immediate concerns of the task to how you can use the task to build mastery.

Boring tasks tend to have high task inertia because they are not exciting. Adding an element of challenge to them can up the excitement, and help them pass by a little more quickly.

What happens if you don't tick all of the items on your list?

I have many days where I don't tick off all of the items on my list. It's a natural occurrence, actually. I plan to do certain things in a day, but I don't always get round to them. Life gets in the way sometimes. Sometimes it is because things take longer than expected, but other days, its because I just struggle to concentrate. We're all human, and we're all going to have days where we don't get to do all of the things we want to do.

If ticking all of the things on my list makes me feel great about myself, it is natural to ask if not ticking everything on my list would make me feel bad about myself. The answer is no, it doesn't. The reason for that is that I know I still tried. I still got some things done, and I still made progress with what is important to me.

My advice to you would be, keep your guilt in check, because it will eat into your productivity. If you don't get everything you wanted done in a day, it doesn't mean anything. It's not an invitation to judge yourself. You can't judge yourself into being productive. At least, not for very long. Shame might make you work a little harder the next day, but it's unlikely to motivate you long enough to accomplish your goals.

Another way of putting it is that there are many paths to accomplish your goals. Choose the one that's a bit more enjoyable. Choose the path where you are kind to yourself, enjoy life a little, and still accomplish your goals. Feel good about what you try to do rather than what you don't do.

Other options

Not everyone likes to-do lists, and that's fine. They work for me, but they might not work for you. What is important is that you take charge of your own productivity, and the things that are barriers to that. If you find your own method that works for you, then great! To help you think, I'll mention a few alternatives.

Book out time in your calendar

Booking out time in your calendar is a popular way of focusing your attention on a particular task for a particular period of time. I do this for my weekly check-ins, for instance. I find that setting aside 30 minutes every week, and having a reminder come up on my phone, helps keep me on track.

Knowing that you have set aside time for a specific purpose can help focus your mind on the task at hand. If you're struggling with productivity, it might help if you keep your sessions short with frequent breaks. After a few weeks of maintaining your focus for the entire session, you could look at increasing the length of a session.

You might set aside some time in the morning to work on that novel. Or perhaps you'll book out two hours in the mid morning to catch up on administrative tasks.

Be conscious of your habits

Every day that you work on changing your habits is a good day - even if you get little real work done. Remember, every time you follow your habit and do some work, you are rewiring your brain to make doing work easier in future. You're working on the habit as much as you are working on the task.

In order to get the most benefit from your habit, you should reward yourself by thinking positive thoughts whenever you engage in your working habit. You want to reinforce this habit, and thinking positive thoughts whenever you engage in it is one good way of doing so. Even if you miss your work target, you are likely doing better than you were before.

At the moment, your task inertia is causing that process to be inefficient and frustrating for you. But if we can change the process, we can rewire your brain, increase your productivity and decrease your frustration. For this reason, it is important to be consistent with your habit, and engage in it every day. The good news is that any time you engage in a productive habit, you are rewiring your brain. In that case, any time you overcome your task inertia and get some work done, even if the amount of work done is small, you can feel good about yourself because you are changing your brain.

No doubt, this sounds odd. We're told to celebrate big successes. We're told to feel good about marathon 12 hour work days, not 15 minutes of productivity. From my point of view, it depends upon perspective. If you struggle to get even 1 hour of real work done in a day, then increasing that to 1 hour and 15 minutes is a victory.

It is a victory that you know you will be able to build on, and that's what makes it empowering. It is the start of change within yourself. You understand enough about task inertia to know why you struggle to be productive, and how to use these strategies to lower you task inertia, change your thought processes, and become more productive.

Therefore, any day that you work on changing your brain is a good day.

Break habits

Its 10AM. You're focused on your work, and making progress. You're solving problem after problem. Then suddenly, you encounter a problem you haven't seen before. Your brain says it, "Let's take a break and get some coffee."

The flow state you were in, where time passed effortlessly, evaporates in an instant. Suddenly you can barely even remember what you were working on. "Okay brain, we'll take a break.", you say, and make yourself a coffee.

But after your well deserved coffee, which you drank outside sitting in the sun without looking at any electronic devices, you try to go back to work. Except... you don't. You check the news quickly. Then your favourite social media site. Before you know it, you're researching what the difference is between a llama and an alpaca.

I'm sure everyone can identify with the above story. We take short breaks, but those breaks can turn into longer breaks. Sometimes when we take breaks, this can cause the faulty working habits to re-engage, and that can make it difficult to get back to work. Especially if there is no deadline, we can find it difficult to feel the urgency that will get us back to work.

What is happening in this case is that we are in flow mode, which is a state of heightened focus and productivity. When we break the flow, we need to get back into it. Sometimes, having an interrupt like a message from a colleague requesting help with something can help us to re-engage flow mode. But, sometimes there is no message waiting for us, and we need to re-engage flow mode on our own. How do we do this?

Time box your breaks

The first thing we need to do is time box our breaks. Set limits on how long your breaks can be, in a way that makes sense for you. There are many ways that you can structure your break routine, and you need to find the one that works best for you and your day.

Some people prefer having 5 minute breaks every hour. Others prefer less frequent, but longer breaks. For instance, you might have a 15 minute mid morning break and a 15 minute afternoon break. Be sure to take time for lunch in addition to rest breaks.

When you time box your breaks, you make an agreement with yourself that you will restart work once the break is over. You could set a reminder on your calendar to remind you to get back to work.

Write down what you were doing before your break

Now that you're back at your desk at the appropriate time, how do you re-engage with work? How do you avoid getting stuck into reading boring articles on the Internet?

One good tip I've discovered is to write down the context of what you were doing before you started your break. This could be in the form of a Post-It note, or it could be a text document that you use. The reason for this is that most of us need a little reminder of the intricate details of what we were doing. We might know the task that we were busy with, but we forget the exact problem that we got stuck on. We forget what we were thinking about in relation to that task.

Writing down your short term memory serves two purposes. The first is that it is a good way to jog your memory, and get your mind back to a state of flow. The second is that thinking about what you were busy with, might cause you to immediately re-engage with the task. This is because it should be the first thing you see when you get back to your desk.

It might still take you a few minutes to get back into a state of flow, but writing down what you were doing should shorten that time considerably.

Tell someone

The last suggestion I have is to tell someone else that you are taking a break. This should create accountability in your mind, as you know that they know that you are taking a break. Therefore, you should feel an urge to get back to work as soon as possible, so that they know you are back.

This is not an ideal solution for two reasons. The first is that it still represents an external management structure - you're relying upon someone else to provide accountability for you. The second is that it works because you would feel guilty if you thought your colleague knew you were not working.

Neither of these are good things for task inertia. Guilt can easily feed into a cycle of stress that will lower your productivity further, and our ideal situation is where you control your own productivity without needing someone else to hold you accountable.

Exercise

Now that you have identified your goals and targets, you need to think about the habits that you'll need to achieve them. Given the above advice, create a habit plan for the week which describes what you will do and when you will do it. Write this habit plan down, and begin implementing it.

Chapter Summary

- Habits are any activity performed with a regular routine.

- Habits are what enable us to reach our defined targets and goals.

- To-do lists can be effective for maintaining habits, but aren't the only option. You can also book out time in your calendar.

- Take breaks as you need them, but take to ensure you can get back into a state of flow after your break.

Chapter 8

Evaluation

If you have got targets and goals setup, and habits to keep you working towards them, you're probably a lot more productive than you were before. You're probably also feeling good about it.

But there might be a nagging doubt in your head - how do I keep this up? How do I ensure that I stick with it, that I don't get sidetracked?

The answer is that you need evaluation because evaluation provides habit reinforcement. This is because of the problem of brittle habits.

There is a lot to unpack there, so we'll start with brittle habits.

Beware brittle habits

A brittle habit is a habit which seems to be going well, until you hit a bump in the road and then you stop performing the habit, resetting your progress to zero. It is frustrating, but it happens, and it can happen with nearly any habit.

I'm sure most of you reading this have tried to go back to the gym. It is all going well, you're making regular visits to the gym and feeling good about yourself, but then something happens. You sprain your ankle. Or you catch the flu. No problem you say, I'll just go back after I'm better.

But you don't. The temporary break from the habit in order to recover from your ailment soon turns into a permanent break, and before you know it, your gym habit is a distant memory.

This is a brittle habit - a habit that you stop engaging in after a small setback. Any habit can be a brittle habit, and we need to recognise this.

My own writing was a brittle habit. I had my daily writing habit worked out. I was writing around 1000 words per day in the morning before doing my job. I did this without fail every morning, with only about 2 mornings off in nearly 2 months.

But over time, my output began to decrease. It started with taking a holiday, actually. During the week I spent away from home, I didn't write. When I came back from holiday, I found it difficult to get back into the habit. My creativity waned, and it became harder to think of things to write. I still wrote, but I'd miss more days. I'd be less productive. Worse, I accepted this decline. I shrugged my shoulders and said, "At least I'm still writing."

I had some leave saved up, and so I took a week's break from work. It might not surprise you that I did little writing in this time. But what I did do, was take daily walks, and on one of those walks, I realized that there was something missing from myself that I had not even noticed was gone. It was my creative expression.

I realized I needed to get things back on track. Writing was too important to me to allow it to fade into the background like that. The habit had become brittle, it had broken, and although I'd picked up the pieces, the habit was barely there.

Habit reinforcement

The problem is that, if the only thing keeping you working is a habit, any break in that habit will usually mean that the habit stops working. There are some exceptions to this. Highly driven people often don't have a problem, but then highly driven people usually don't identify as suffering from task inertia either.

Almost all habits are brittle to a degree, and you need to be aware of this before you start working. Although many habits are brittle, we can work around this by building systems that reinforce the habit, in order to keep us on track.

Habit reinforcement refers to creating another system to reinforce the habit that you want to be productive at. It should involve having a higher level view of what you are busy with and what your progress is. You should also not perform your reinforcement habit on the same routine as your productive habit. This is because, if you stop your productive habit, you will likely stop your reinforcement habit too.

You need to keep your reinforcement habit going even if your productive habit stops. Luckily, your reinforcement habit need not be overly time consuming to be effective. Thirty minutes once per week is all that it should take to get a good view of how productive you have been and whether you are on track with your goals.

Self-evaluation

Self-evaluation is one example of a good system for reinforcing a habit. By taking time every week to evaluate your progress, you can prevent yourself from slipping out of a habit or breaking it entirely. Evaluation allows you to pause, and think about where you are now and where you are going.

During a self-evaluation session, you should be engaging your higher level, long term thinking. You should be taking a longer view of your life, and your general mental state.

I believe that all aspects of our lives are more closely linked than we think. Therefore, while I think it is important to think about your goals while doing a self-evaluation session, you'd be wasting it if that is all you thought about. You should also be evaluating other aspects of your life, such as your physical health, emotional wellbeing, and relationships.

This is not to say that you should hold your relationships up to a harsh light and scrutinise them. But it does mean that you should acknowledge their importance in your life.

Having a greater awareness of these aspects of your life might give you insight into things you need to work on, possibly things unrelated to your goals. If nothing else, one needs the physical and emotional energy to pursue goals, and so looking after your physical and emotional health is crucial for continued progress. You might also find yourself feeling happier and more at peace, as you elevate your thinking out of the mundane day to day activities and into more exciting possibilities.

You can do your self-evaluation in different ways. I have a routine that works for me, which you are welcome to borrow, or otherwise develop your own that suits you better. I like to do my self-evaluation on Sunday evening. I sit down with my computer and evaluate myself in a few categories - Summary, Physical Health, Emotional Health, Career, Writing and Financial Health. Your categories might look different to mine - adjust them to suit your needs. I don't have a separate Relationships category - given that Relationships have such a large influence over my emotional health, I prefer to write about relationships there. But you might want a separate category depending on your approach to life, and possibly if you are married.

I don't use numerical scores for my evaluation. I write down how I felt, why I felt that way, and what was going through my head. I find that writing this down forces me to think about how I am really feeling, and this is a very helpful tool for determining whether you are on track or whether you are slipping.

I keep a record of my evaluations, but I don't expect to go over them later. The important part of the evaluation

139

process is not the record keeping, but the check-in with your feelings.

You might not need to keep a record of your evaluations, but I do recommend that you either write down your self-evaluation, or have it in the form of a dialogue with a trusted coach or mentor. The reason for this is what when we articulate our thoughts into words, we clarify them. Communicating your feelings in either written or spoken form will force you to delve deeper than if you spent 30 minutes thinking about where you are.

Coaching

Performance coaching is another example of a system for reinforcing a habit. A performance coach would be someone that you report your progress to, but who is not necessarily interested in the results of your work. In other words, you are accountable to a performance coach but not responsible.

The difference between a manager and a coach would be that a manager needs the output of the work you are producing, whereas the coach simply wants to make sure that you are still productive for your own sake. A coach can be a professional that you hire, but it could also be a friend or family member that you trust.

Having a coach that you regularly report progress to will inspire you to get your work done, and may be a good means of reinforcing your productive habits. This is especially true for productive habits that you engage in that are not tied to your employment, if you are employed.

Many of you might be wondering, if there is some overlap between coaches and managers, why it is that people with managers are still often not as productive as they would like? The answer is that having a manager creates a powerful incentive to bend the truth with regards to your productivity.

Because productivity is often so important to our egos, and because none of us would like to be accused of being lazy, we don't like to admit to our managers that we were not productive. We might admit that a task took longer than expected, but we are not likely to say that this was because we struggled to focus, or were distracted by social media. We fear judgment for admitting that we were unable to focus enough to be productive.

This is partially because we know that our job performance is continually being evaluated. The results of this evaluation influence any external rewards we might receive, such as promotions or salary increases. We aren't dishonest about productivity problems because of the economic consequences, but rather, because we wish to still have the good feelings that come along with praise and recommendations for a promotion or a raise. On the other hand, depending on the labour law in the country where we work, we might reasonably be worried about dismissal for low performance if we admitted to having productivity problems.

I don't wish to excuse dishonesty, but neither do I want to pass judgment on people for productivity problems. There are many causes of productivity problems, few of which are due to pure laziness. As I've said, only chronically unproductive people can be said to be lazy, and lazy people would likely not bother to read a book about productivity.

With a coach, this is not an issue. A coach cannot recommend you for a promotion or a raise, no matter how productive you are. Neither can they recommend you for dismissal, even if you admitted to watching YouTube videos for 8 hours straight.

Therefore, we have less incentives to be dishonest with a coach. Even so, it must be emphasised that a coaching relationship can only work if a great deal of honesty and trust is present. If you're dishonest to your coach, you're being dishonest to yourself.

Be kind to yourself

One thing you need to realise before starting any process to improve your productivity is that you will have days or even weeks where you are not productive. We are all human, and sometimes life can get in the way. You might get sick, injure yourself, or simply become distracted because of a new relationship. It can all happen, and frequently does.

If you're unable to forgive yourself for lapses in productivity, you'll find that this makes your habits more brittle, not less. While having high standards for yourself can be motivating, you need to allow for the occasional lapse in productivity.

The reason for this is that being too hard on yourself tends to create excessive guilt, and this guilt can further lower productivity. I'll use the example of a new gym routine to illustrate this point.

Suppose that you had recently started a new gym routine. You have been doing it for a month, and have seen great improvements in your fitness and energy levels. You also like the way it makes you feel about yourself. But you catch the flu. It isn't the worst flu you've ever had, but its enough to put you out of action for a day or two. During that time, you skip gym classes. Not only are you worried about making other people sick, but you are also aware that your body needs time to rest in order to beat this infection.

But once you have recovered from the flu, you might find that excuses start to pile up. You don't feel ready to go back, or, you're so busy with work that you don't have time today. Soon, it's a week since you have recovered, and you haven't been back. Then you realise it is a month since you last went to the gym.

This is a frequent occurrence with most types of habits. The cessation of habit that occurs can simply be because you took a break. Sometimes that is all that it takes to disrupt a habit. However, guilt frequently makes this more likely to occur.

This is because we tend to think that being harder on ourselves will make us more likely to engage in the habit. However, this same hardness in our approach can increase the brittleness of the habit, because when a break occurs, we aren't resilient enough to get back where we left off. We don't forgive ourselves and get back to the habit, instead, we silently admit failure and move on.

You need to forgive yourself for lapses. They will happen. You will have days where you are too stressed, too sick or too busy to work on your personal projects. You will have days where high stress levels or sickness compromise your productivity in your primary job. When that happens, and it will, you need to be forgiving towards yourself for it.

If you're too critical of yourself for these lapses, it might actually cause what you fear, which is the cessation of the habit. You might rather break the habit altogether than admit you can't keep up the same pace of work every day. Allow yourself to be human, and to have human problems, and bounce back to your work rather than leave it altogether.

If you need a break from a productive habit, I recommend sticking with your regular evaluations. If, during an evaluation, you feel that you have done less than you would have liked, forgive yourself and resolve to try again. You might want to think about lowering your targets a little, in order to work on building the habit back up again.

But if you've got this far, that the brittleness of a habit is even something you think about, then you know that you can resume the habit anytime that you like. You're not in a race with anyone to finish that book first - it is a marathon where you are the only entrant.

Evaluation

Give some thought about how you will reinforce your new habits. What scheme would work for you? Create a scheme that will keep you on track. I recommend booking time out in your diary immediately to ensure you stay on track.

Chapter Summary

- Beware brittle habits! A brittle habit is one that ceases at the first interruption.

- Use self-evaluation or coaching to reinforce your habits.

- Realise that you are only human, and can't maintain 100% output 100% of the time.

Chapter 9

Managing task inertia in others

You now know how to recognise and manage task inertia in yourself. You know of some strategies that can be helpful for dealing with it. You now know that productivity is not as simple as motivation or laziness. You have a more detailed understanding of how motivation and task inertia combine to influence productivity.

You might find that you view the productivity of others differently after reading this book. I hope you have a more nuanced understanding of what affects productivity. If you're managing other people, perhaps you would like to use what you have learned to help you get the best out of your colleagues.

While this book is not intended to cover all aspects of management, I will offer some advice to managers on how to apply task inertia theory to their colleagues. This advice is aimed at people managers who have direct reports, rather than other types of managers who do not.

Establish a dialogue

It would be nearly impossible to improve productivity without a trusting relationship established with your colleagues. Without trust and openness, you won't know what is going on in the lives of your colleagues, and they won't feel comfortable telling the truth about how they feel working with you.

Regular, open and honest communication is required to build up a trusting relationship with your colleagues. I'd advise one on one chats scheduled every 1-2 weeks, in addition to line of business communication that occurs in the course of the week.

Don't Assume

The most important thing that you can take from task inertia theory is not to assume you understand the reasons why a particular employee is unproductive. There might be many such reasons, and by assuming you know the answer, you're just likely to make the employee defensive.

While earlier chapters of this book were devoted to categorising people according to how task inertia influences their productivity, it is important that you apply this to yourself only, and not others. Making assumptions about what drives another's productivity will lead you to make mistakes with no potential upsides. Rather let the employee tell you themselves what they are struggling with.

You can use the insight that you have gained reading this book to assist your colleagues, but offer that as insight instead of judgment. Remember that productivity is a very sensitive subject in the workplace, and if the employee perceives that you may be judging them as unproductive, they might trust you less and be less open with you.

Therefore, when you communicate about productivity with your colleagues, don't make assumptions about why their productivity is as low or as high as it is. There may be additional stresses occurring in the home, or elsewhere in the employee's personal life, that you are not aware of. Any assumptions about whether task inertia is or is not involved could be wrong and will likely be seen by the employee as judgment.

Don't judge

It's natural to get frustrated when a previously reliable employee is taking longer than usual to complete a task. You might start to wonder whether you underestimated the complexity of the task, or whether the employee is not being as productive as they used to.

It is important that you do not attach a negative judgment to productivity going down. Perhaps the complexity of the task was not underestimated, and perhaps the employee really is not very productive at the moment. This can and does happen. Nobody can sustain 100% productivity 100% of the time.

One way of looking at this would be to say that we should not judge others in general, because we don't know what they are going through. I wholeheartedly agree with that, and I'd encourage you not to judge others. But I know this may fall on some deaf ears where productivity is concerned. You're paying them to do a job, after all. Shouldn't they just do the job?

The logic is sound from a certain point of view, but another way of looking at it is that attaching a negative value judgment to productivity issues can only make them worse, not better. If you're really after getting as much productivity as you can from your colleagues, then a negative value judgment is not going to help you get there.

Using negative emotion to motivate people to work will only motivate them to work just hard enough not to get fired. You will never get their best, most creative selves, because they won't feel comfortable expressing them around you. Moreoever, they won't feel that you deserve their best selves - and they'd be right.

Connecting with Don't Assume above, you should neither assume you know why an employee has been unproductive, nor attach a negative value judgment to your perception of their productivity.

Aim for happiness and you'll get productivity

There is a clear link between productivity and happiness. Happy colleagues who are engaged and fulfilled by their work will be more likely to be productive and even go the extra mile. Employees who feel unappreciated will do the bare minimum required of them - sometimes even less than that.

Given that this book is about productivity, it might be tempting to say that one should discuss productivity with the employee. In my view, this would be a mistake. If you inform your colleagues that you only want to increase productivity, you might be sending the message that their happiness is not important to you, and what is important is their output. Needless to say, this might make them feel unappreciated.

If you assist your colleagues in feeling appreciated, engaged and fulfilled by their work, their productivity will increase as a byproduct, and you will enjoy a trusting relationship with your colleagues.

You can discuss productivity with your colleagues, but you need to be sensitive about it. This is because discussions about productivity can frequently be taken as accusations of laziness. If an employee feels that they are being accused of being lazy, they will become defensive and probably not engage with you further on the subject.

Until the taboo around discussing productivity in the office is broken, it is wise to be wary how you discuss it.

Instil a culture of improvement

Given that a lot of this book has been about recognising the causes of productivity problems, its natural to assume the same should apply when managing others. The issue with doing so is that you may create what you seek to eliminate.

If you define everything in terms of problems and solutions, you may lower your colleagues confidence. You may make them think that you believe they are not productive. Imagine how you would feel if your boss said to you, "We need to work on your productivity problems", when you did not think you had any! This relates to both Don't Judge and Don't Assume. You would be doing both if you said that colleagues needed to work on their productivity problems.

This is where having a dialog with your colleagues can help. You'll get a better feel for what they think about productivity. You'll know how motivated they feel. You'll have some empathy for them.

This does not mean that you should not help solve productivity problems when they do occur. It just means that you should be careful about phrasing your intent. If you ask a colleague how they are finding their role, and they mention productivity problems, by all means, help them solve them.

Act as a facilitator and a coach and guide them through the process of solving their own productivity problems.

Some working disciplines have regular retrospectives which aim to improve various aspects of the working process, such as productivity or quality of output. Such retrospective sessions would be an appropriate place to bring up productivity, as long as it is not targeted at a particular employee. The benefit of this is that the organisation continues to improve, even if that improvement is only localised to your team. After all, there is no perfect system of working. Even if you have the right system of working at the moment, it might not be optimal once conditions change. Therefore, encouraging regular retrospectives, and using that feedback to drive a process of change and improvement, can keep your system of working aligned with the current conditions.

Tell your colleagues about the vision

If you're a manager, you're likely making decisions which have a longer term impact. You're likely privy to information about the vision, objectives and roadmap of your organisation that your colleagues do not have. Depending on your position, you may even be deciding some of these things yourself.

I established earlier that short term thinking is a hallmark of task inertia. If you don't have your eyes on the horizon, you're unlikely to be thinking of much else other than how your tasks make you feel. If you're susceptible for task inertia, this can cause it to become more noticeable.

Therefore, you should communicate what the long term vision and objectives are to your colleagues, and help them understand why the work that they are doing now is important in the long term. This will help them place their work in the larger context, and may make them feel that it matters.

This is also good practice as far as trust and openness goes - it shows that you value your colleagues enough that you would trust them with information about the long term plans of the organisation. Having been there myself, its frustrating when you are working on something and you have no idea how this fits into the organisation. You're essentially looking at it from a black box perspective, working on mystery tasks with no understanding how these relate to the larger whole.

Sharing this information with your colleagues will demonstrate trust to them, and may enable them to lower their own task inertia by focusing on the organisational objective.

Help your colleagues plan for their futures

You know the importance of long term goal oriented thinking in overcoming task inertia. Therefore, to help your colleagues overcome their task inertia, if they have any, you could help them think of the future. In the context of the workplace, we're referring to the future of your employee's career.

Many companies, even some surprisingly large ones, will tell you that their career framework is coming out "next week". It has been coming out "next week" for the past year, and is still not done. While the career framework is not done, your colleagues may have little idea where they can advance in the organisation, or what the requirements for doing so are.

This is an unfortunate and unfortunately all too common scenario, but it does not excuse you from helping your colleagues plan their futures. Since you should be having frequent one-on-ones with your colleagues, you should be discussing career planning with them. You might not be able to give them the official position on where they can go and how they can get there, but you can help them start thinking about what they want. Make sure to guide them through the process of connecting what they want - their goals - with the work that will help them get there - their targets.

Some colleagues are mindful enough that they have their own career plans that they are working towards - which may or may not involve remaining in your employment. But many are just working their roles day to day, with little thought about the next step. As I've said, the problem with this is that short term thinking is a hallmark of high task inertia.

Without thinking about the future and then connecting that to tasks performed in the present, task inertia is likely to rear its head, and cause frustration.

Therefore, its important to discuss career plans with your colleagues, and connect work done in the present with plans for the future.

Of course, career goals are heavily dependent upon the person, and not everyone strives to become the next CEO. However, a personal growth trajectory need not include greater and greater responsibility - it could include a greater sense of satisfaction with one's work, or increasing mastery. Connecting the positive future, whatever that may be, with the employee's current workload is a good way reduce task inertia.

Help colleagues take responsibility

It is true that the road to recovery from task inertia is realising that your productivity is in your control, and also that you don't have to love your job in order to do it. However, communicating this to colleagues directly may send the message that you are not supportive of them as people.

Taking responsibility for your own productivity can be a difficult concept to communicate clearly. First, there is the possibility that your colleague may think you are accusing them of laziness. As already mentioned, this will shut down further attempts at helping your colleague.

But, another issue is that it might be difficult for someone who suffers from high task inertia, to internalise such advice. If they take responsibility for something because you tell them to, have they really taken responsibility for it? After all, your end goal is for them to succeed in whatever they wish to, even if they leave your employment and work elsewhere.

If that isn't what your end goal is, then you should consider your motivations more clearly.

Therefore, subtlety is likely necessary. I'd suggest asking your colleagues how you can help them be more productive. You aren't accusing them of being unproductive, with all that entails, you are asking how you can support them and further their ambitions. They will then need to come up with suggestions that they believe will help them be more productive.

Don't be surprised if the answer is "nothing". Going back to Don't Assume, you should not assume that your colleague believes that there is a problem in the first place.

Chapter Summary

- Build trusting relationships with your direct reports - any productivity improvement at all requires this.

- Don't assume you know why a colleague is not productive, and don't attach a negative value judgment if you think they are not productive.

- Aim for happiness and you'll get productivity.

- Help your direct reports with long-term career planning.

- Help colleagues take responsibility for their productivity, with subtlety.

Conclusion

It is hard to believe that I am writing this, and it is still 2020. Earlier this year, I was a wreck. I felt wretched about myself, and I was not productive at all. I felt like I was letting myself down and not living up to my potential. It is now the end of November 2020, and I am writing the conclusion to the first book I have published in my life. In my Google Drive are drafts of fiction works that were started this year, two of which are over 10000 words long. My productivity in my day job has returned to normal levels, despite not having a manager looking over my shoulder. I am able to get my work done within the hours that I allocate for it.

It certainly was not enjoyable, being pushed to my limits by events out of my control. But, that led me to understand task inertia, and come up with solutions for it. This has led to an incredible change in my life. The stress and guilt reduction alone is simply incredible.

My journey is not done yet. As always, change takes time, and sometimes I fall back into my old ways. I am, after all, only human. But I understand the problem for the first time in my life, and even if I don't always get things right, I know what I have to do. This gives me hope.

This book was written because it is the book that I wish I had to help me through lockdown. It is intended to guide others through the process of taking back control over their productivity, hopefully without the anguish that I went through.

By reading this book, you now understand what task inertia is. You understand that it is the mental resistance that most of us feel when trying to work. You understand that it is possible to be motivated, and still struggle to work. But perhaps most importantly, you see your work habits as slightly more distant from yourself and your worth, and will stop judging yourself – and others – for them.

You have started down the path of taking responsibility for your work habits, by making choices about what you do, in full knowledge that you might not find that inspiration you are craving. That is okay – inspiration is over valued in any case.

You know how to set goals, targets and habits, and keep yourself on track even when life inevitably intervenes.

I hope that reading and understanding this book is as empowering for you as writing it was for me.

Printed in Great Britain
by Amazon

55217597R00097